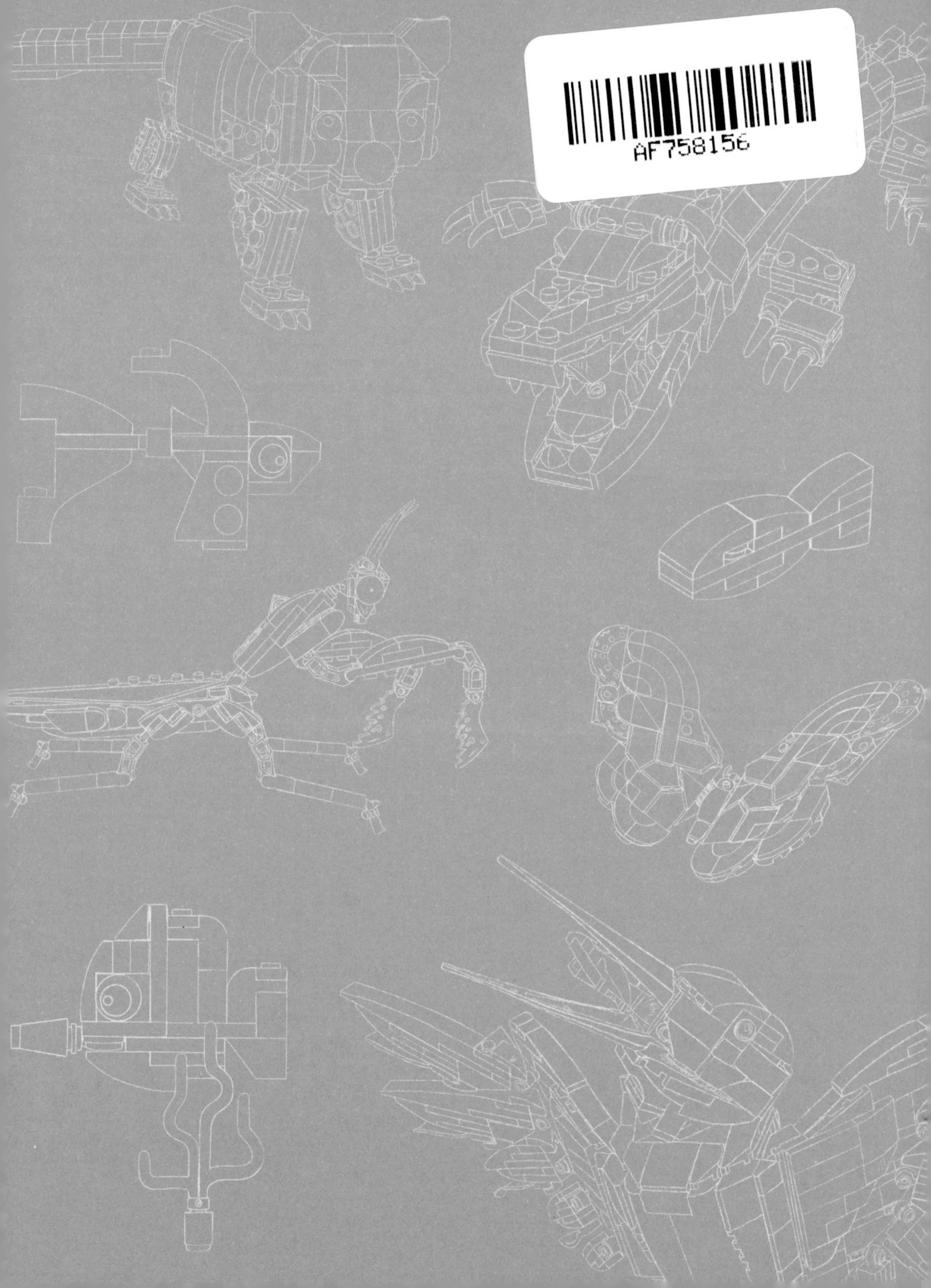

LEGO

Animal Field Guide

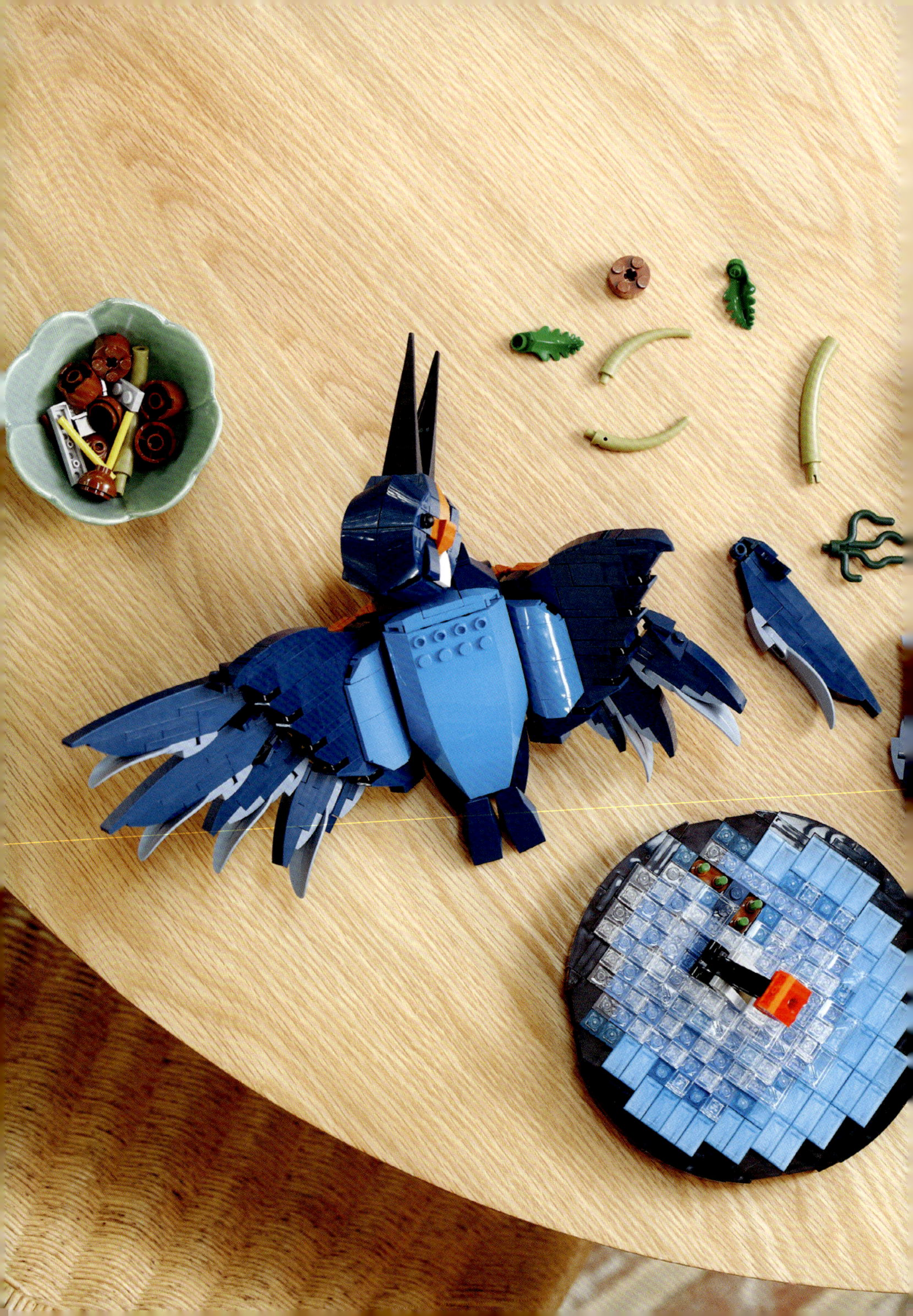

Animal Field Guide

Discover LEGO® Wildlife Big and Small from Around the World

Illustrations by Nina Pace

CHRONICLE BOOKS
SAN FRANCISCO

 Manufactured by Chronicle Books, 680 Second Street, San Francisco, CA 94107 under license from the LEGO Group. Made in Shanghai, China, April 2026.

Library of Congress Cataloging-in-Publication Data available.

ISBN 978-1-7972-4033-6

Manufactured in China.

MIX
Paper | Supporting responsible forestry
FSC www.fsc.org
FSC™ C008047

Illustrations by Nina Pace.
Design by Naomi Desai.
Art Direction by Phoebe Liu.
Photography © 2026 by the LEGO Group.
Text by Mara Nelson-Greenberg.

10 9 8 7 6 5 4 3 2 1

See the full range of LEGO® books and gifts at chroniclebooks.com/LEGO.

Chronicle books and gifts are available at special quantity discounts to corporations, professional associations, literacy programs, and other organizations. For details and discount information, please contact our premiums department at corporategifts@chroniclebooks.com or at 1-800-759-0190.

Chronicle Books is represented in the UK and Europe by Abrams & Chronicle Books, 22 Ely Place, London EC1N 6TE, abramsandchronicle.co.uk, and Média-Participations, 57 rue Gaston Tessier, 75166 Paris CEDEX 19, media-participations.com.

Chronicle Books LLC
680 Second Street
San Francisco, California 94107
chroniclebooks.com

Contents

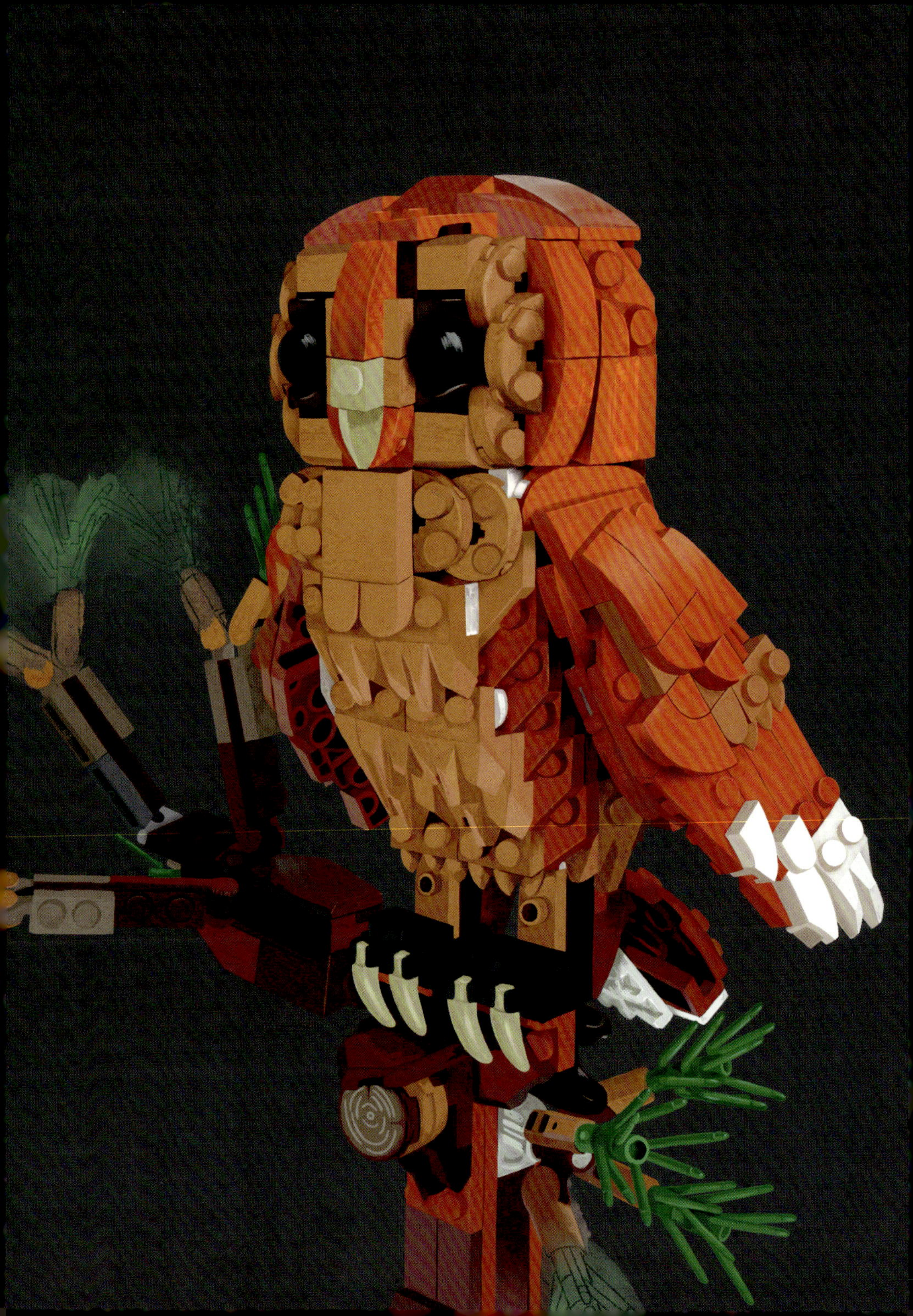

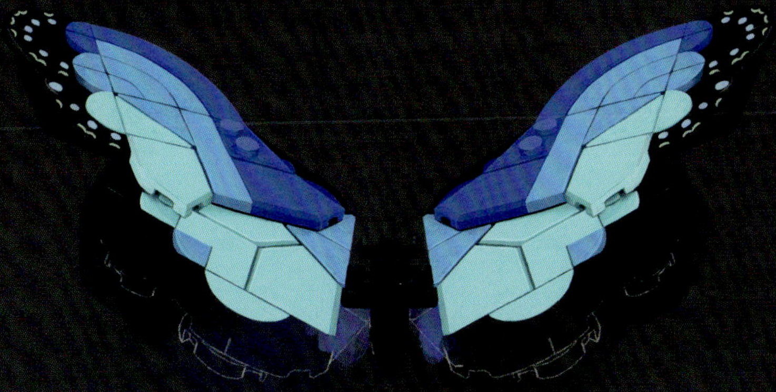

Forests

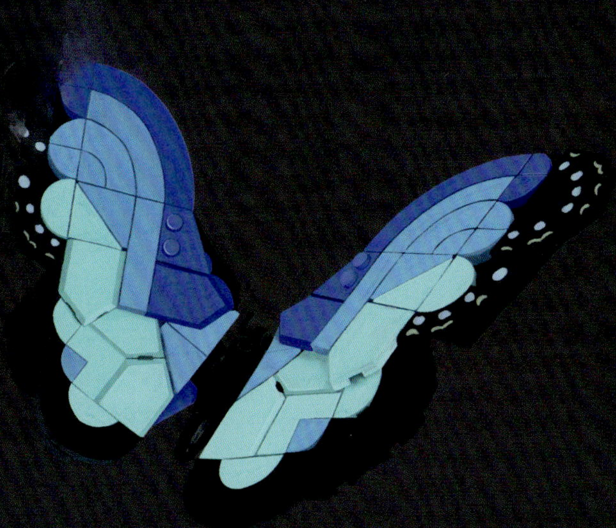

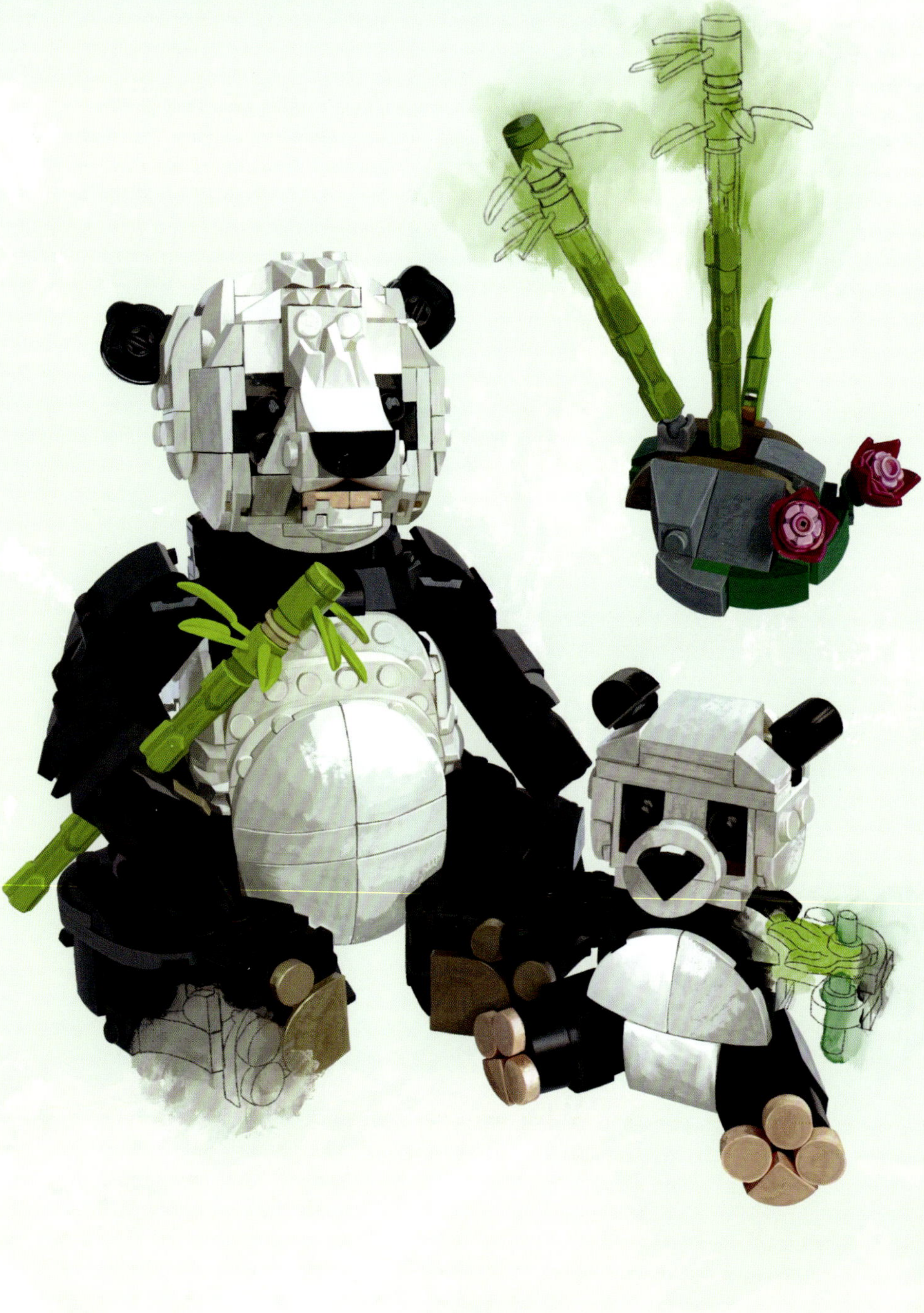

GIANT PANDA

Ailuropoda melanoleuca

Primary Location: Southwest China
Primary Food Source: Bamboo
Average Length: 4 to 6 ft (1.2 to 1.8 m)
Average Weight: 220 to 250 lb (100 to 113 kg)

Giant pandas are beloved across the world, and especially in China, their native home. Although they are the face of many conservation organizations, they are technically no longer classified as endangered, thanks to conservation efforts—but they are still considered vulnerable. Giant pandas are omnivores, but 99 percent of their diet is bamboo. They eat dozens of bamboo species in the wild and use their enlarged wrist bone—which functions as a kind of false thumb—to grip the bamboo as they eat. They are solitary animals and rarely encounter one another in the wild, but they still communicate fairly often, using scent markers to share information like age, gender, and territorial claims.

- *Besides bamboo, the remaining 1 percent of the giant panda's diet consists of meat, fish, eggs, and more.*
- *Giant pandas spend up to 16 hours a day eating and consume up to 31 lb (14 kg) of bamboo daily! As a result, they poop up to 40 times a day!*

GIANT PANDA

Ailuropoda melanoleuca

BONUS INFO AND FUN FACTS!

Newborn giant panda cubs are about 1⁄900 the size of their mothers. They are born pink and hairless, and for the first few weeks of life they cannot see or hear, relying entirely on their mother for food and protection. When cubs are born, the father is not involved in their care—male giant pandas leave after mating—but the mother stays by their side, nursing them frequently and leaving only for short feeding outings. Cubs usually remain with their mother for 18 to 24 months.

- *Giant pandas have a limited ability to taste meat. They're missing the umami taste receptor, which is a protein on the tongue that responds to certain savory flavors.*
- *The giant panda's bite is among the strongest of any carnivore of similar size! Giant pandas have those big, round faces because their jaws need to be big enough to eat all that bamboo.*
- *Unlike other bears, giant pandas don't hibernate in winter. In fact, they don't have permanent dens at all. Instead, during colder months, they simply move to warmer territories.*
- *Raw bamboo contains cyanide, a deadly poison—which makes it an unlikely candidate to make up an animal's entire diet! Giant pandas have developed cyanide-digesting microbes and other natural defenses so they can eat raw bamboo without getting sick.*

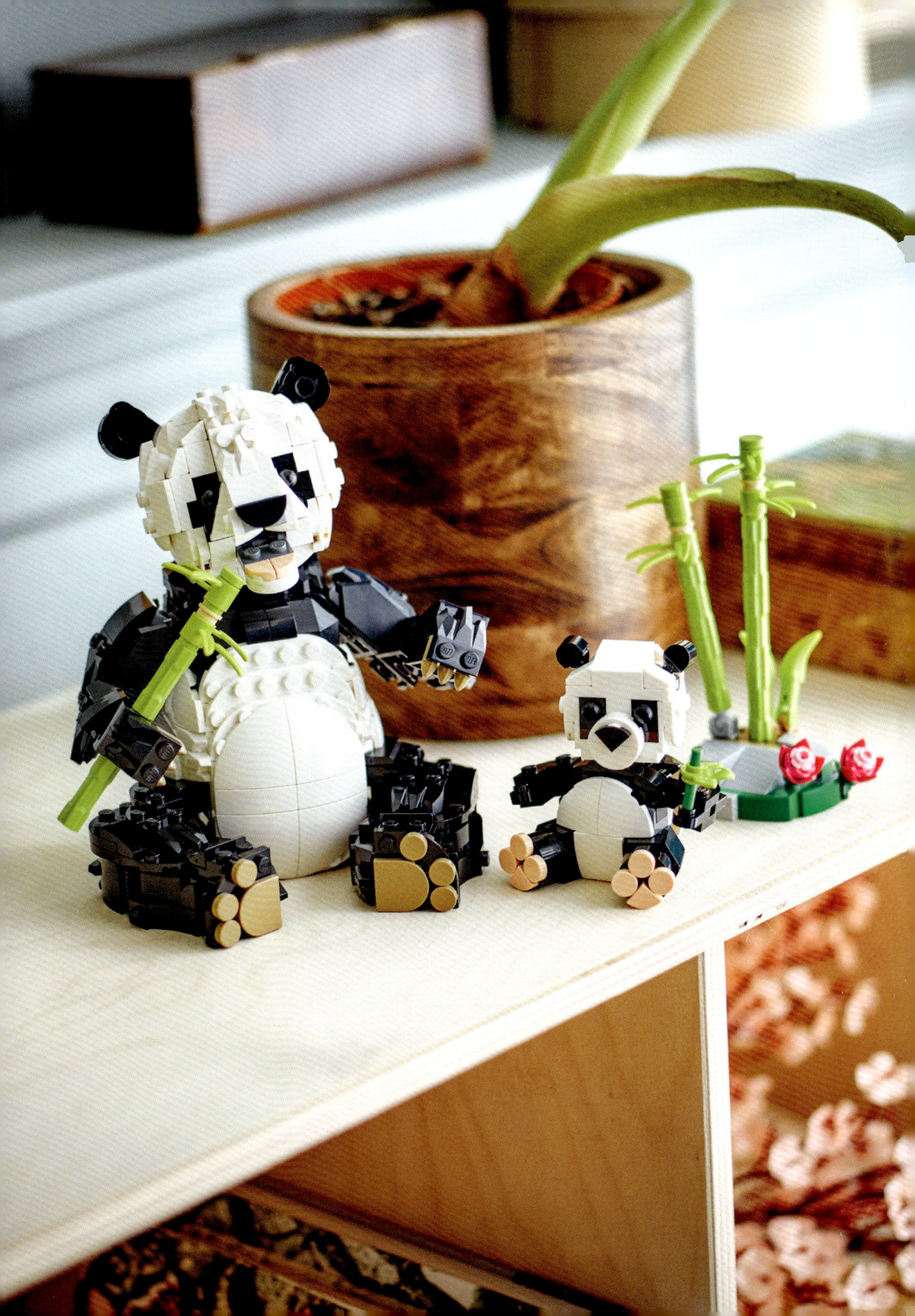

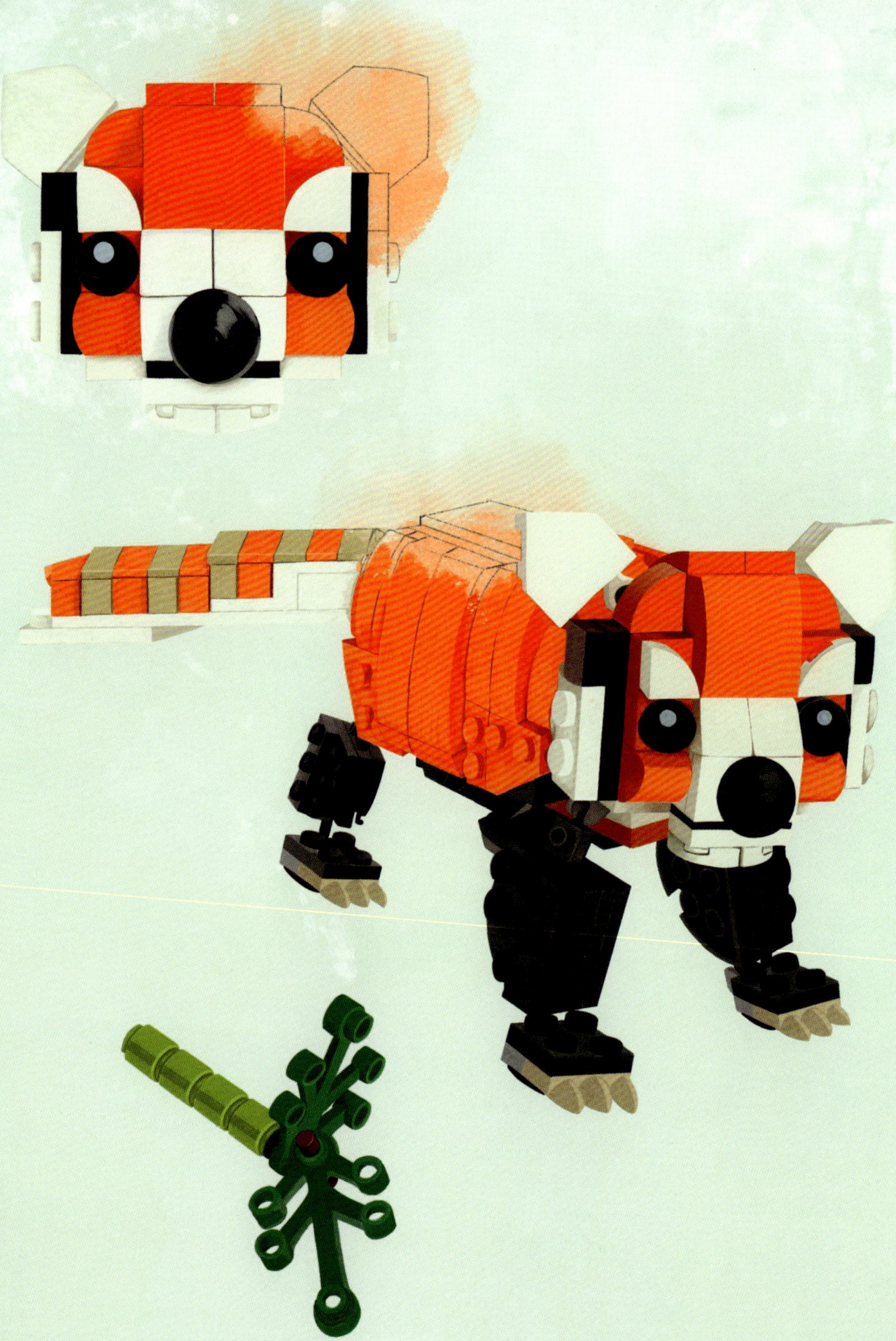

RED PANDA

Ailurus fulgens

Primary Location: Eastern Himalayas and surrounding regions
Primary Food Source: Bamboo and leaves
Average Length: 20 to 26 in (50 to 65 cm)
Average Weight: 6.5 to 14 lb (3 to 6.2 kg)

These adorable animals live mostly in trees close to water sources. They are both solitary and shy. For this reason, much of their behavior has been studied while they're in captivity rather than in the wild. Believe it or not, red pandas actually aren't closely related to giant pandas. The two species don't have a lot in common—except for their enlarged wrist bone, which functions as a kind of false thumb to help them grip! Genetic evidence suggests that red pandas are actually more similar to raccoons, weasels, and skunks.

- *Red pandas need to eat at least 2 to 4 lb (0.9 to 1.8 kg) of bamboo every day. In some cases, that's almost a third of their body weight!*
- *Red pandas have an uneven way of walking, sometimes described as waddling. Can you guess why? It's because their front legs are shorter than their back legs!*
- *A red panda named Futa became a celebrity in Japan for being able to stand up on his hind legs for 10-second intervals. This unusual feat even landed him a role in a soda commercial!*

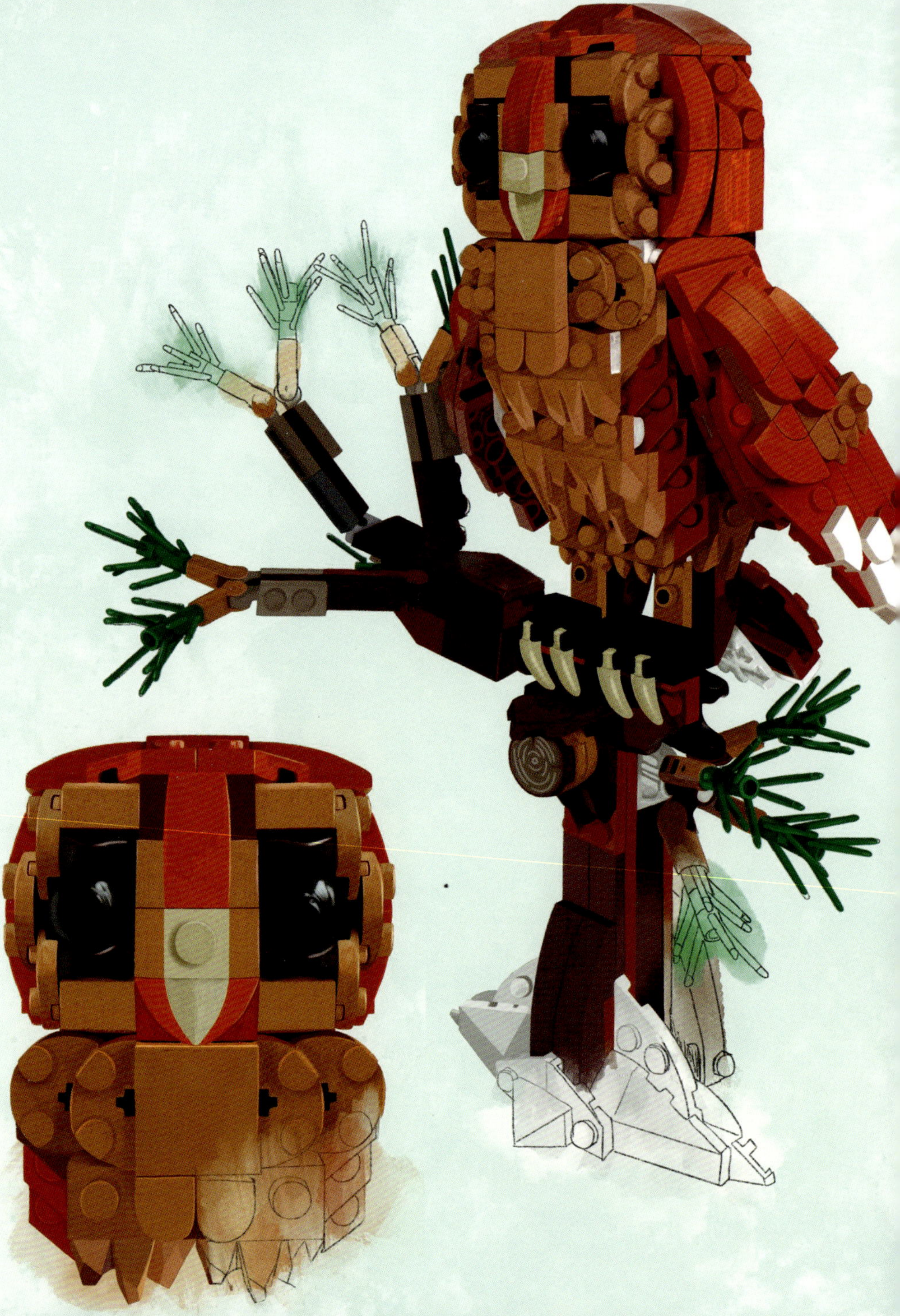

TAWNY OWL

Strix aluco

Primary Location: Europe and parts of Asia
Primary Food Source: Small mammals, birds, and invertebrates
Average Length: 15 to 18 in (37 to 46 cm)
Average Weight: 13.5 to 28 oz (385 to 800 g)

Like many owls, tawny owls can't move their eyes and have to turn their heads to see. While their eyesight is relatively good in low light—definitely better than a human's—they rely even more on their exceptional sense of hearing to capture their prey. They owe their good hearing to their asymmetrical ears: The left ear opening is higher than the right, and the right ear is larger and points downward. Tawny owls are silent flyers, so their prey often doesn't realize they are being attacked until it's too late—the tawny owl has already grabbed them with its sharp talons!

- *The iconic sound that most people attribute to all owls—"too-wit too-woo"—comes from the tawny owl! This sound is actually a call-and-response: The female tawny owl calls out "ke-wick," and the male responds with "hoo-hoo."*
- *Human beings can re-create the call of the tawny owl by cupping their hands together and blowing through a slit between their thumbs. Try it!*

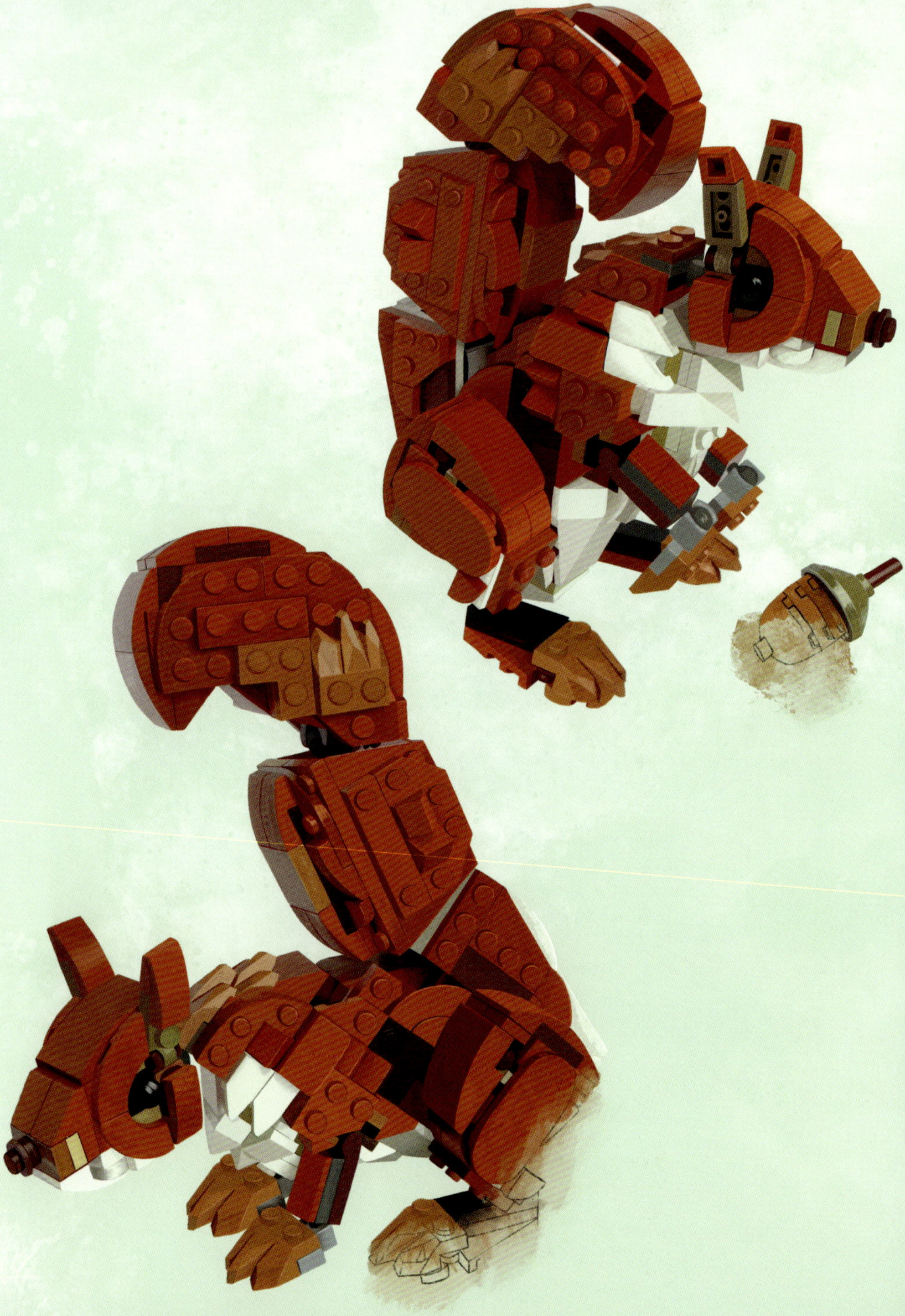

RED SQUIRREL

Sciurus vulgaris

Primary Location: Europe and Northern Asia
Primary Food Source: Seeds, acorns, and nuts
Average Length: 7 to 9 in (18 to 23 cm)
Average Weight: 9 to 11 oz (252 to 308 g)

Fluffy-tailed red squirrels spend most of their time in trees, where they build nests on branches and inside tree cavities. Like many other squirrels, they carry food inside their mouths, then move it to their nests for longer-term storage. This allows them to create food caches that help them survive the winter. Besides seeds, acorns, and nuts, they also eat birds' eggs, vegetables, garden flowers, and sometimes even tree sap.

- *Rather than growing to a set length, the red squirrel's incisors just grow and grow—without stopping! Red squirrels gnaw on hard nuts, bark, and more to help wear their teeth down.*
- *Red squirrels do their part to help out Mother Earth. When they inadvertently spread some of the seeds from their caches around the forest, it helps with forest regeneration.*

RED SQUIRREL

Sciurus vulgaris

BONUS INFO AND FUN FACTS!

These energetic animals tend to live solitary lives, and they are highly territorial—using rattles and screeches to defend their nests and feeding areas from one another. Female red squirrels raise their offspring alone, and the young usually leave the nest after 45 days. However, they don't always strike out on their own right away; young squirrels are sometimes known to study and imitate the behavior of older squirrels to learn how to forage and avoid predators.

- *Red squirrels have double-jointed ankles that can rotate 180 degrees! This makes them great climbers and jumpers.*
- *The red squirrel's bushy tail is a literal lifesaver! Red squirrels can survive long falls from trees thanks to air resistance, their small bodies, and their big tails, which help cushion the landing.*

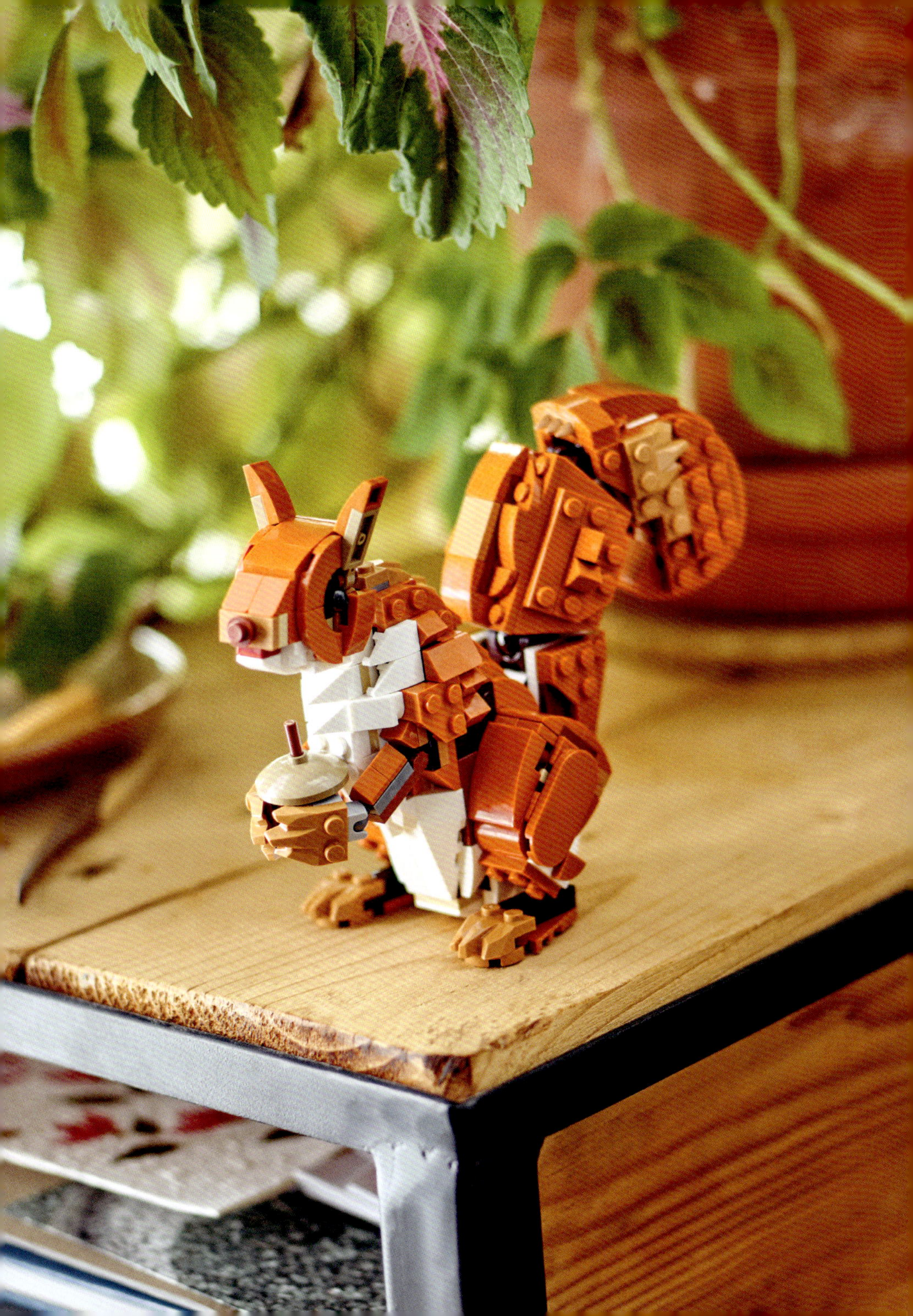

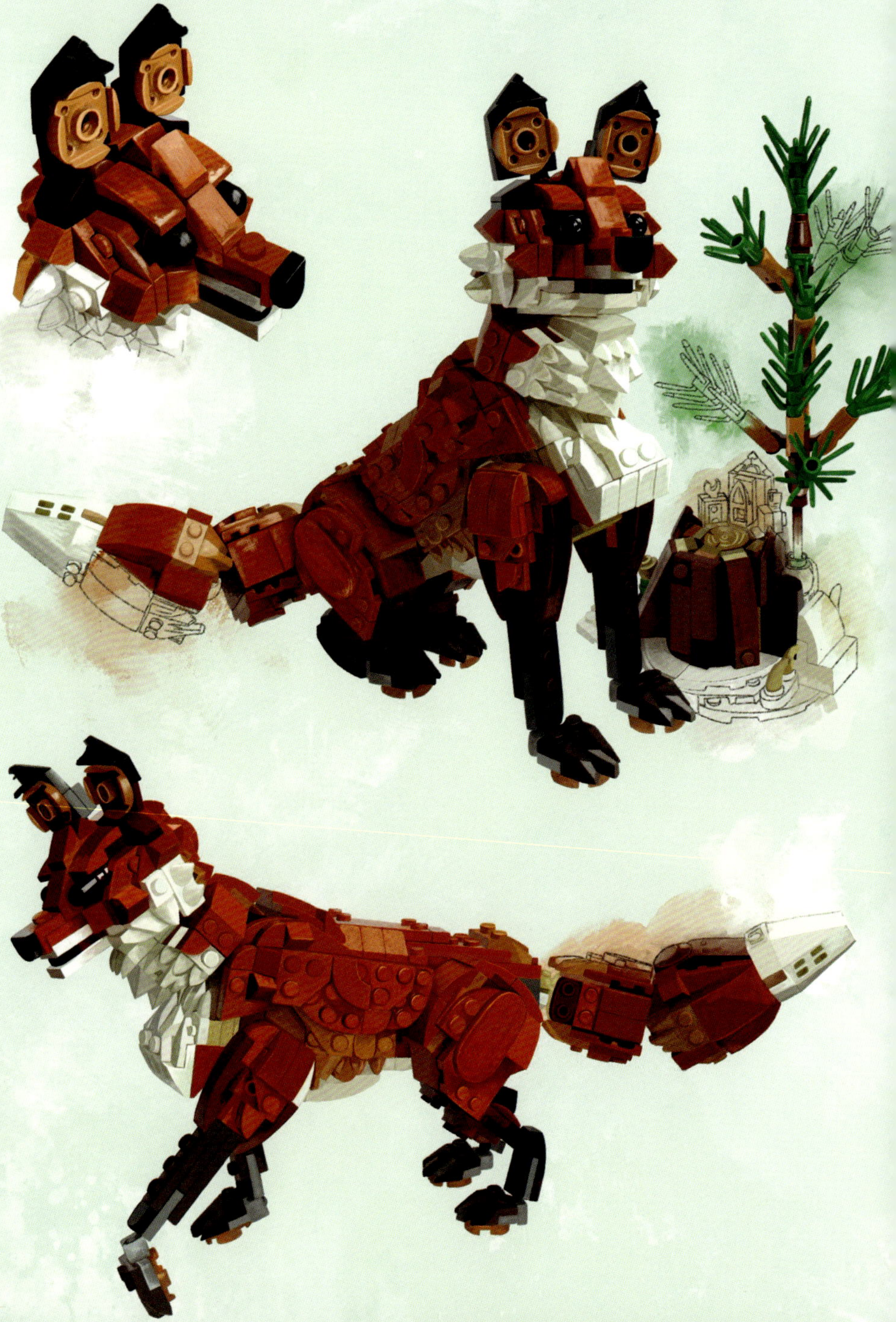

RED FOX

Vulpes vulpes

Primary Location: Across the Northern Hemisphere
Primary Food Source: Small mammals
Average Length: 18 to 35 in (46 to 90 cm)
Average Weight: 6 to 15 lb (2.7 to 6.8 kg)

Red foxes are familiar to most of us from folklore and mythology—they have appeared in Greek mythology, European folklore, Japanese mythology, and Chinese folktales, among others. They are one of the most widely distributed wild carnivores in the world, able to survive in forests, grasslands, deserts, mountains, tundras, and even urban areas. This kind of adaptability can be attributed in part to their varied diet—they've been known to eat over 300 animal species (and many plants as well).

- *A red fox can hear mice squeaking from about 100 ft away. That's more than the length of a basketball court!*
- *Red foxes have an extra digit on their front paws to help them with gripping and digging. Their front paws each have five digits, but their back paws only have four.*
- *Let's get these guys to the opera! Red foxes communicate with sounds that span five octaves. That's at least two more octaves than the average human vocal range!*

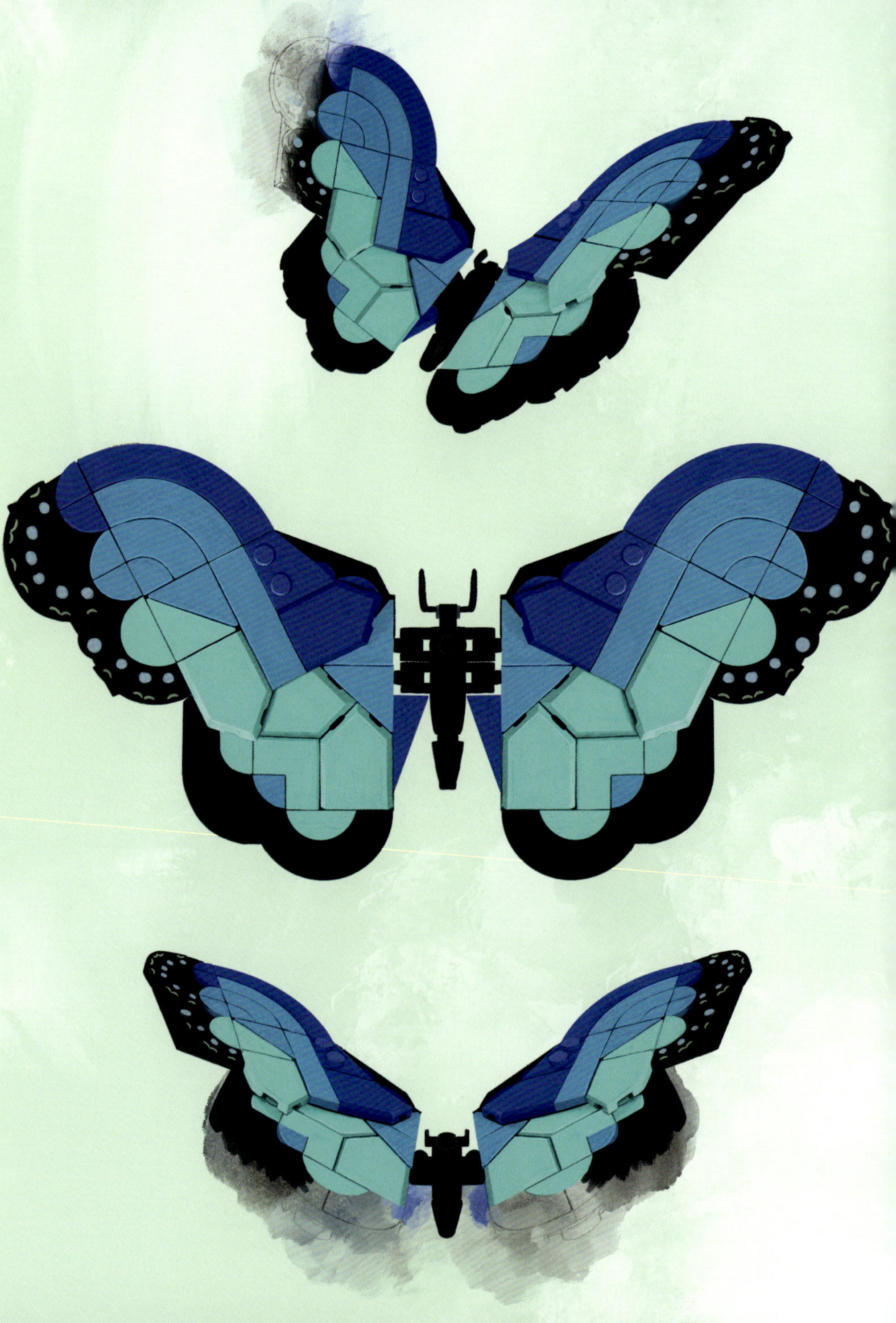

MENELAUS BLUE MORPHO

Morpho menelaus

Primary Location: Central and South America
Primary Food Source: Rotting fruit, tree sap, and fungi
Average Length: Wingspan of 4.7 in (12 cm)
Average Weight: Lightweight; not well-documented due to butterfly physiology

Blue morpho butterflies are known for their striking blue color, the result of light bouncing off tiny scales on their wings. Their wings also have eyespots—special markings that resemble animal eyes—that blue morphos use to confuse and scare off predators. Their wings are so structurally complex that scientists study them in the hopes of improving our own technological designs.

- *Blue morphos don't taste fruit with their tongues—they taste it with sensors on their legs!*
- *Humans are often drawn to the blue morpho's beauty, making them popular among collectors.*

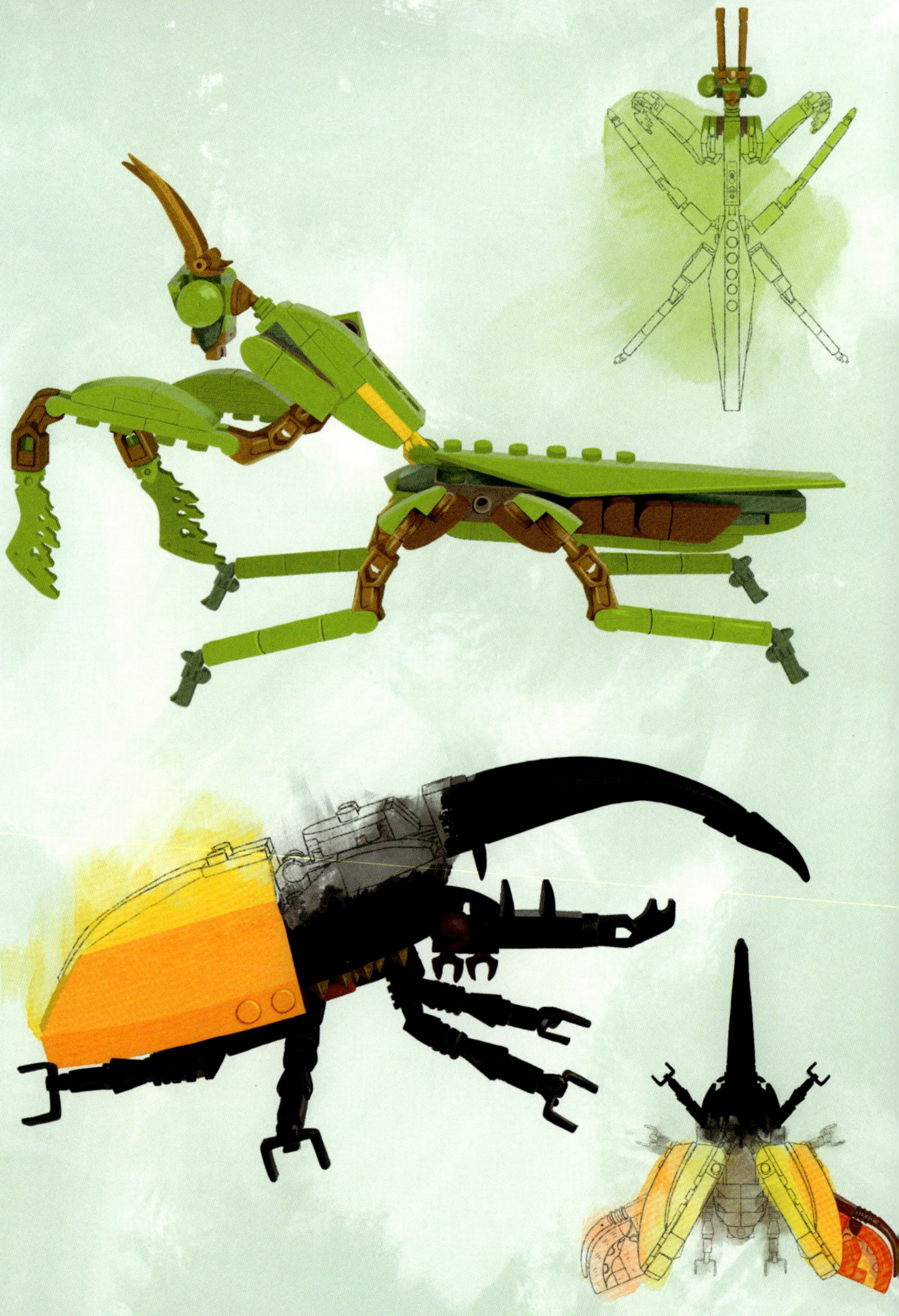

PRAYING MANTIS

Mantis religiosa

Primary Location: Europe, Asia, Africa, and North America
Primary Food Source: Insects and other small animals
Average Length: Up to 3 in (7.5 cm)
Average Weight: 0.1 to 0.2 oz (4 to 5 g)

The *Mantis religiosa*—also known as the European praying mantis—can be tan, bright green, or many shades in between. The name *mantis* comes from a Greek word that means "prophet," and mantises are known for standing still on their hind legs with their forelegs raised—a position that looks a bit like meditation or prayer. Despite their calm appearance, they're deadly carnivorous predators. Adult female mantises can eat prey that is significantly larger than they are, like reptiles, amphibians, and hummingbirds.

- *Praying mantises are famous for an odd mating behavior: After mating, the female mantis will sometimes kill and eat the male!*
- *Look again! Praying mantises have a pseudopupil—it may look like they have pupils, but the dark spot near the middle of their eyes is actually an optical illusion, caused by the way light interacts with their compound eyes.*
- *Not one, but two well-known martial arts styles were inspired by the movements of the Chinese praying mantis!*

HERCULES BEETLE

Dynastes hercules

Primary Location: Central and South America
Primary Food Source: Fresh and rotting fruit, and also tree sap
Average Length: Up to 7 in (17 cm)
Average Weight: 0.41 to 1.32 oz (11.6 to 37.4 g)

Hercules beetles are the longest beetle on Earth, if you include their horns. Their horns make up more than half their body length, and male Hercules beetles use them to fight other males for the attention of female beetles. During this unusual mating ritual, Hercules beetles will pick up and throw one another with their horns.

- *Do you know how the Hercules beetle got its name? From its strength! A Hercules beetle can carry hundreds of times its own weight.*
- *One person's trash is a beetle's treasure! Hercules beetles are known to eat rotting fruit, tree sap, and decaying wood.*

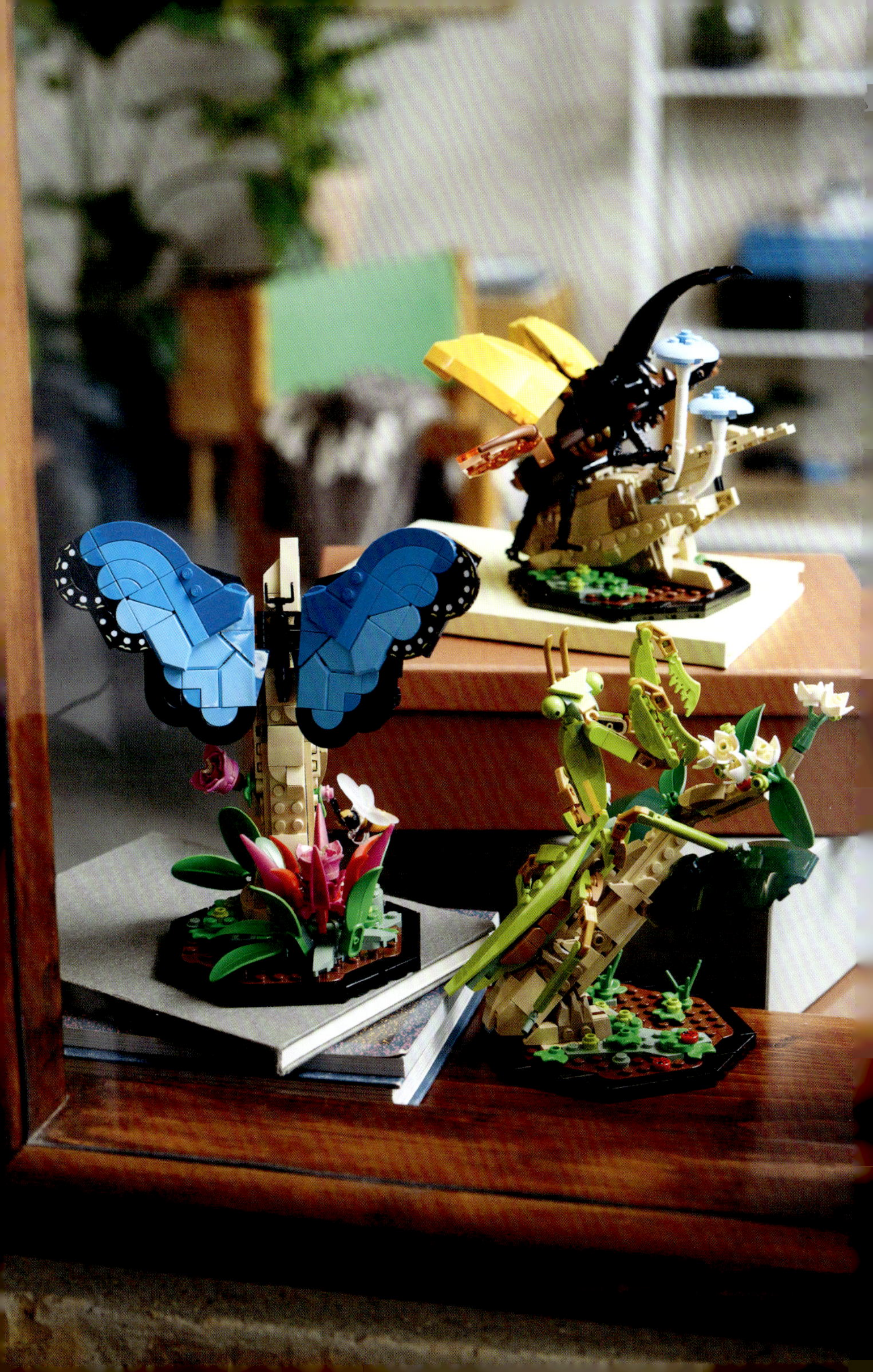

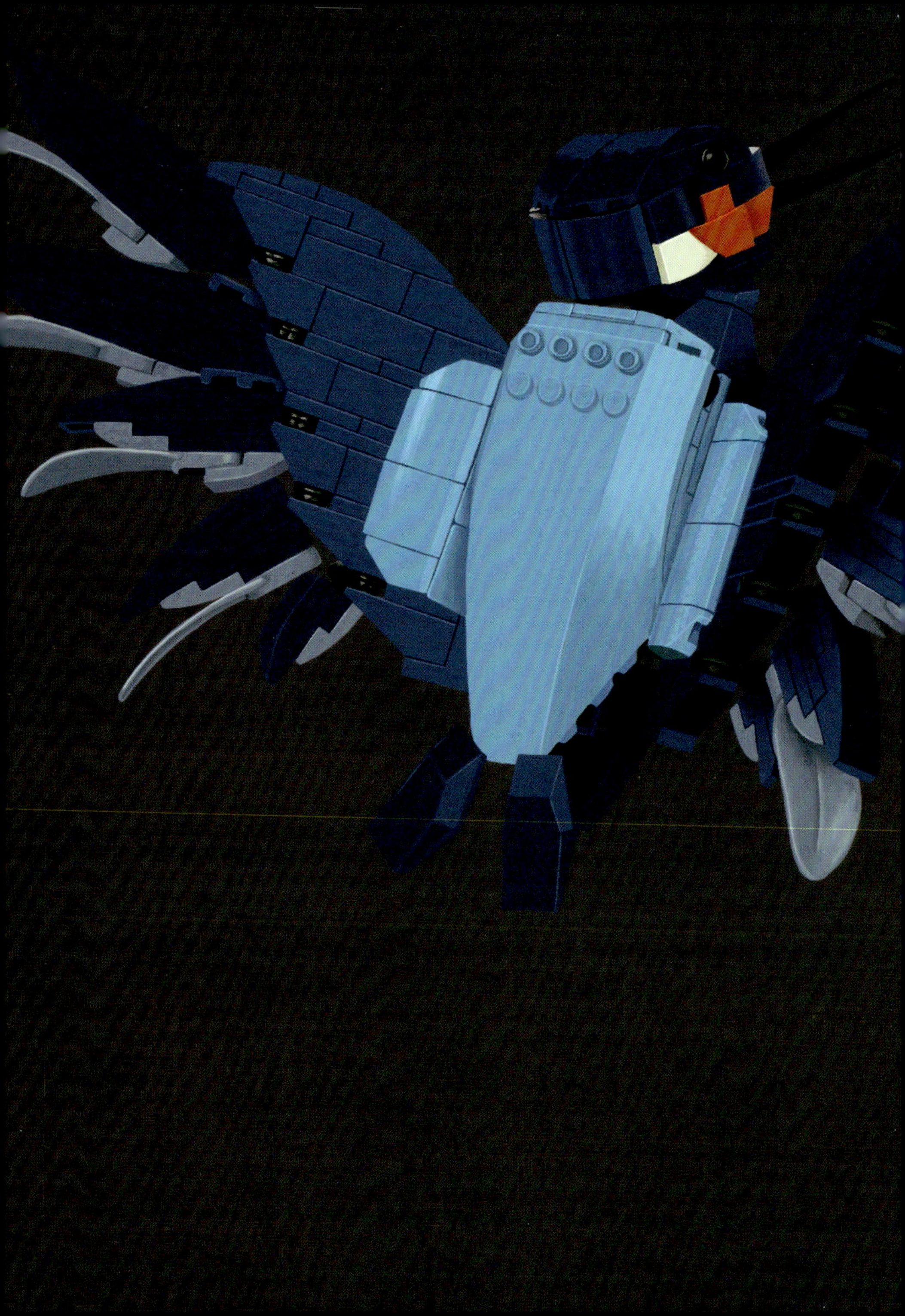

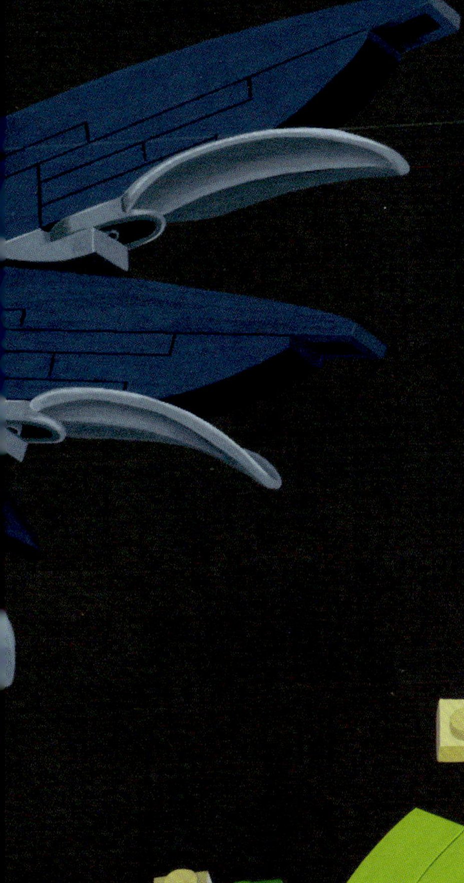

Tropical Rainforests

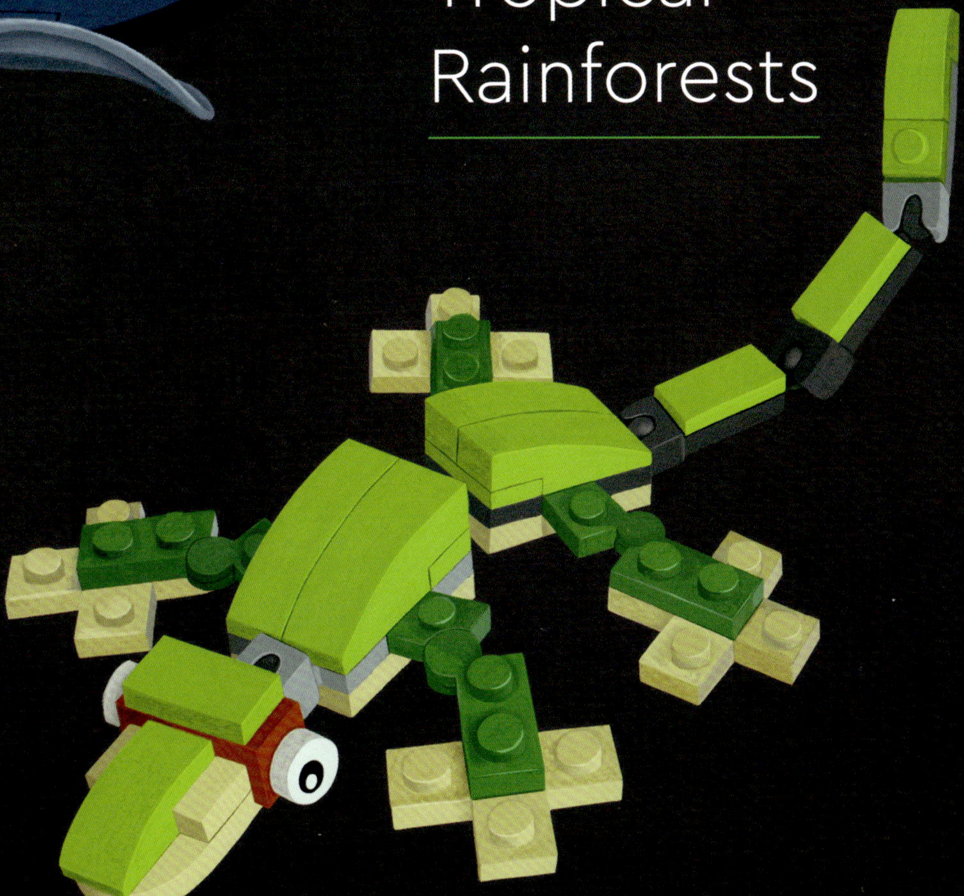

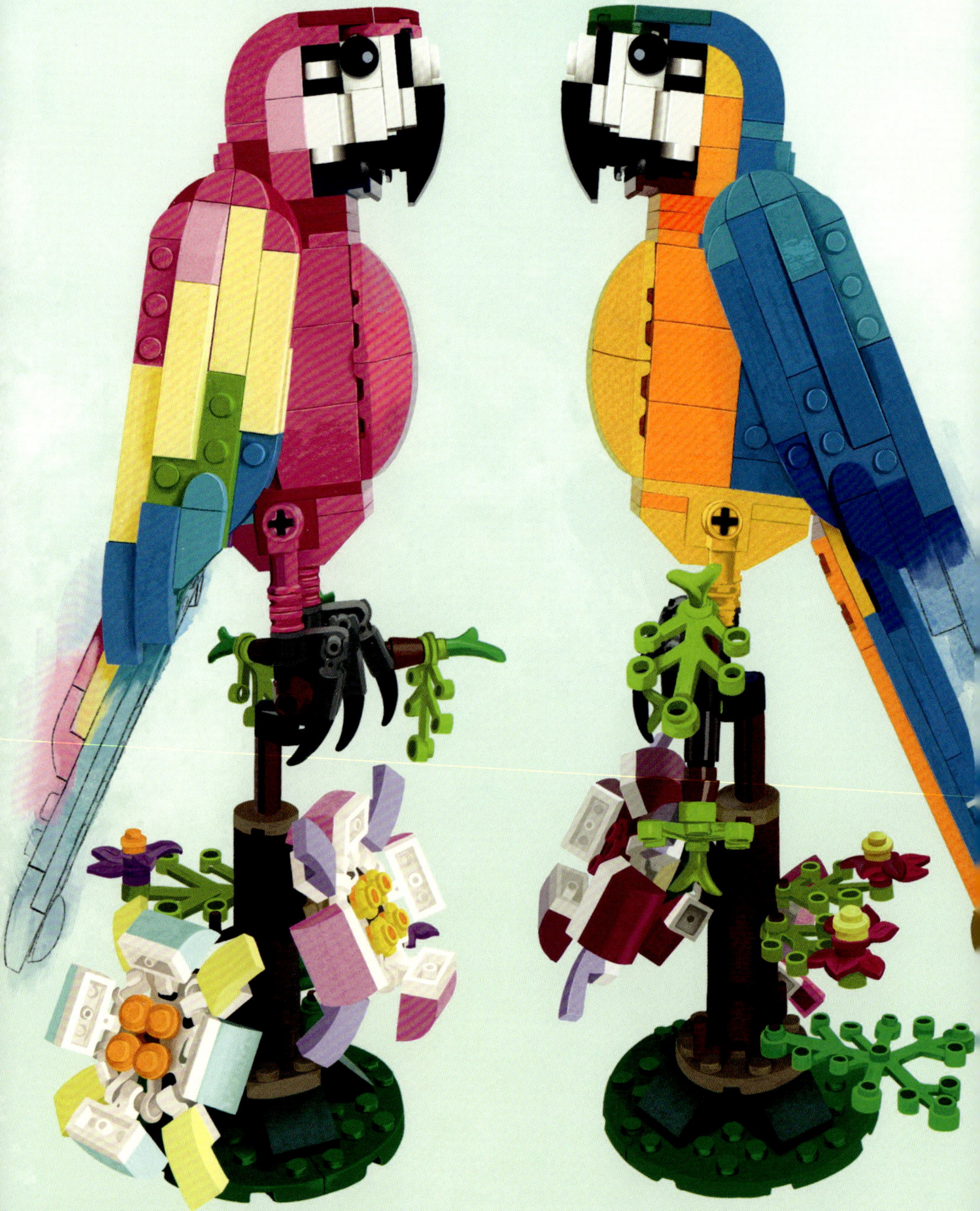

BLUE-AND-YELLOW MACAW

Ara ararauna

Primary Location: South America
Primary Food Source: Seeds, nuts, fruit, and vegetation
Average Length: 30 to 34 in (76 to 86 cm)
Average Weight: 2 to 3 lb (0.9 to 1.4 kg)

This blue-and-gold parrot is one of the most popular pet parrots in the world thanks to their beautiful feathers and uncanny ability to mimic human speech. It's estimated there are one million blue-and-yellow macaws in captivity. In the wild, parrots can live up to 30 years, but in captivity, they live even longer—blue-and-yellow macaws sometimes live more than 60 years. Scientists have not yet discovered any species of pink macaw, but with a little bit of LEGO® creativity, you can build new animals of any color you like into existence. Can you spot the subtle differences between the two builds?

- *It's true love! Most parrots in the wild stay with one mate for their entire lives. They fly so close together that their wings nearly touch—even when they're traveling with a large flock.*

- *Researchers often study wild birds by attaching tags or bands to them. But do you know why it's difficult to do this with parrots? They chew those markers right off!*

- *Blue-and-yellow macaws eat various fruits and plants—and also clay! Scientists think the clay might provide minerals to supplement the birds' diet or help counteract the toxins found in unripe seeds.*

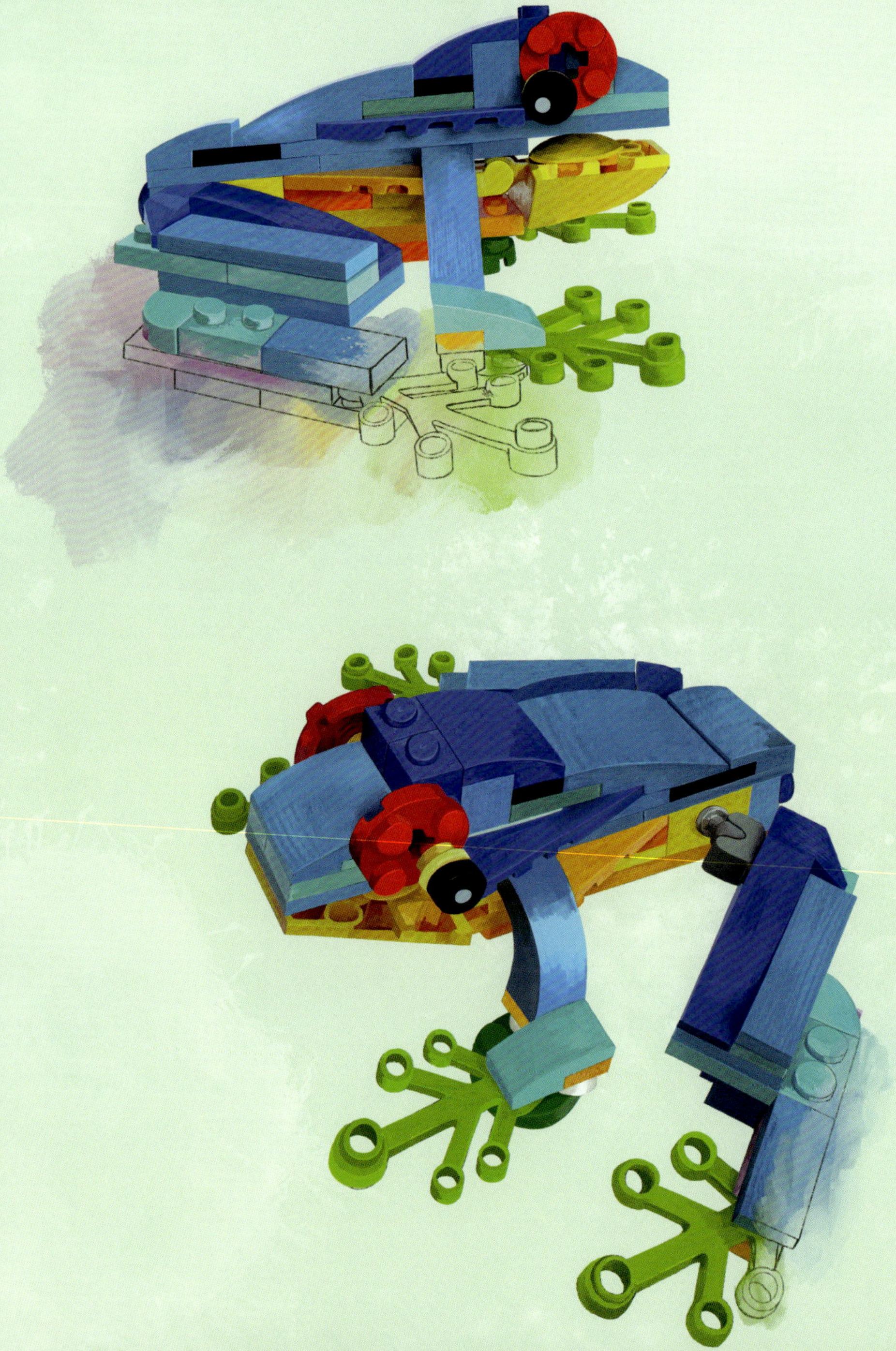

RED-EYED TREE FROG

Agalychnis callidryas

Primary Location: Central America
Primary Food Source: Insects
Average Length: 2 to 3 in (5 to 7.5 cm)
Average Weight: 0.2 to 0.5 oz (6 to 15 g)

Red-eyed tree frogs have a striking appearance: red eyes, orange feet, and bright green backs with blue and yellow striped sides. The LEGO Red-Eyed Tree Frog doesn't have quite the same coloration—but the inspiration is clear in the large red eyes. In the rainforest, red-eyed tree frogs blend into the leaves thanks to their green backs and smooth skin. When they close their eyes, the red is hidden, allowing them to further blend into their surroundings. They also have a thin membrane over their eyes in addition to an eyelid. This allows light in so red-eyed tree frogs can sense an approaching predator even when their eyes are closed. If a predator *does* come near them, they will flash all their bright colors! This sudden burst of color startles the predator, giving the frog time to escape.

- *Red-eyed tree frogs hatch their eggs on leaves directly above the water so their tadpoles can drop right in! The tadpoles will live in the water for weeks or even months.*
- *Red-eyed tree frogs protect themselves by feeling vibrations. When their embryos feel a vibration around them that is specific to certain predators, they will seek out safety by hatching early and falling into the water.*

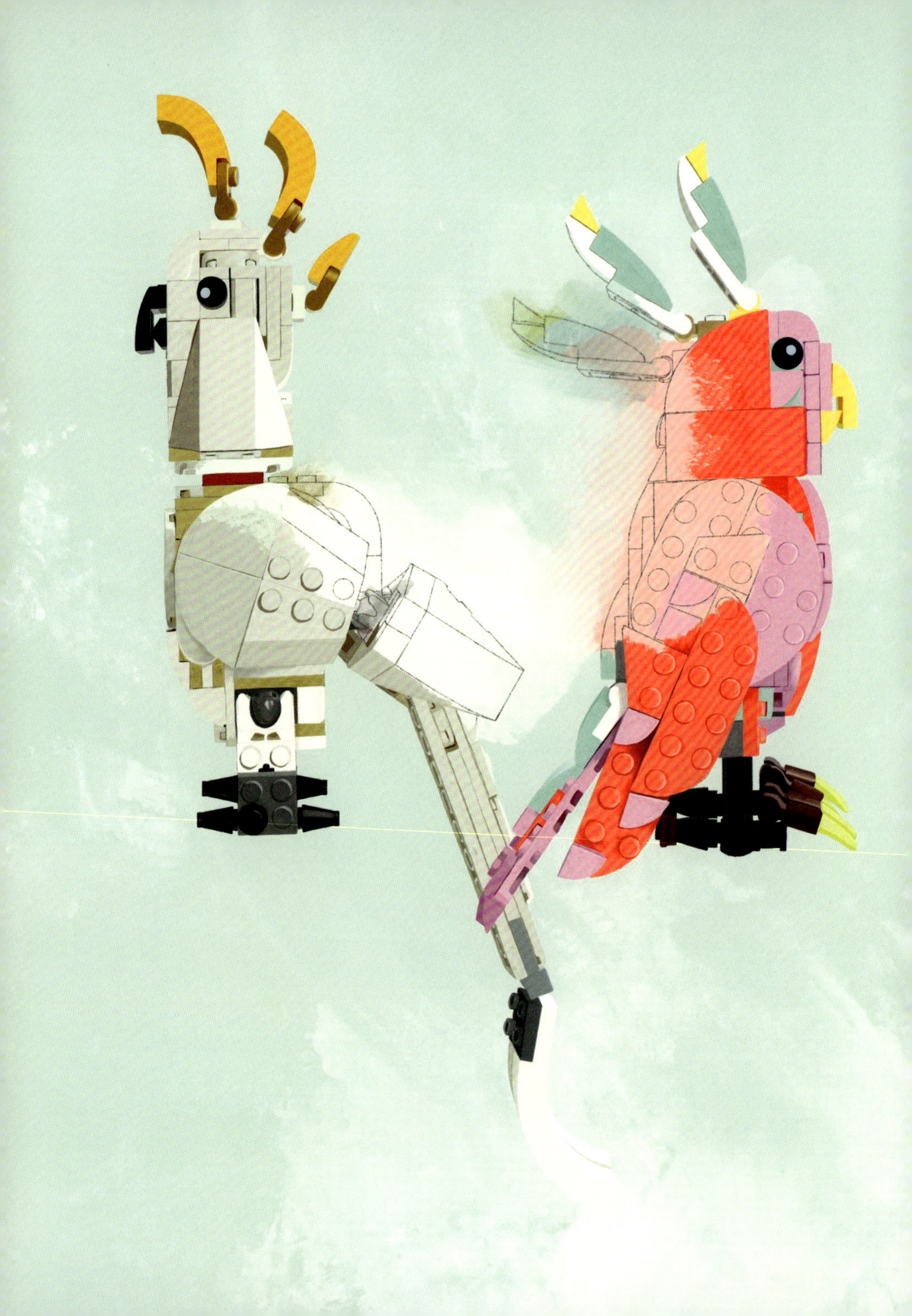

SULPHUR-CRESTED COCKATOO

Cacatua galerita

Primary Location: Australia and New Guinea
Primary Food Source: Seeds, nuts, fruit, and roots
Average Length: 17 to 21 in (44 to 55 cm)
Average Weight: 28 to 40 oz (800 g to 1.2 kg)

Sulphur-crested cockatoos can dance! Their ability to synchronize their movements with music and adjust those movements based on tempo was discovered when a sulphur-crested cockatoo named Snowball was seen dancing along to the Backstreet Boys. To this day, Snowball still holds the Guinness World Record for most dance moves by a bird: 14 recorded moves ranging from the "downward head bob" to the "headbang with lifted foot" to the "semicircle low head sweep."

GALAH COCKATOO

Eolophus roseicapilla

Primary Location: Australia
Primary Food Source: Seeds, grains, nuts, and roots
Average Length: 14 in (35 cm)
Average Weight: 10 to 14 oz (300 to 400 g)

The galah cockatoo is one of the most widespread bird species in Australia. They travel in big flocks ranging from 10 to 1,000 birds! While male and female galahs look very similar, you can identify them by their eyes: The male galah's irises are a very dark brown, almost black, while the female galah's eyes are a lighter brown or red.

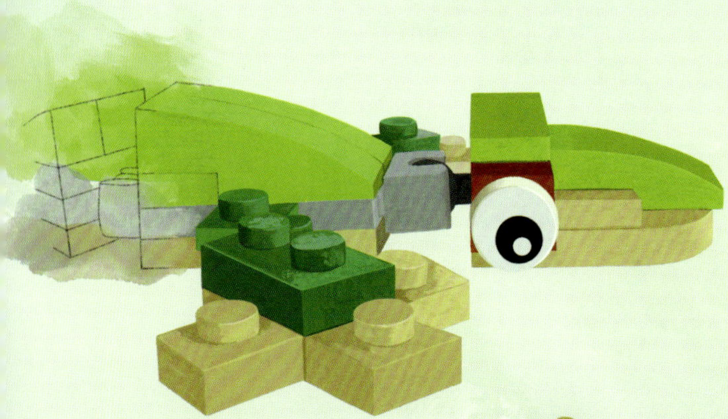

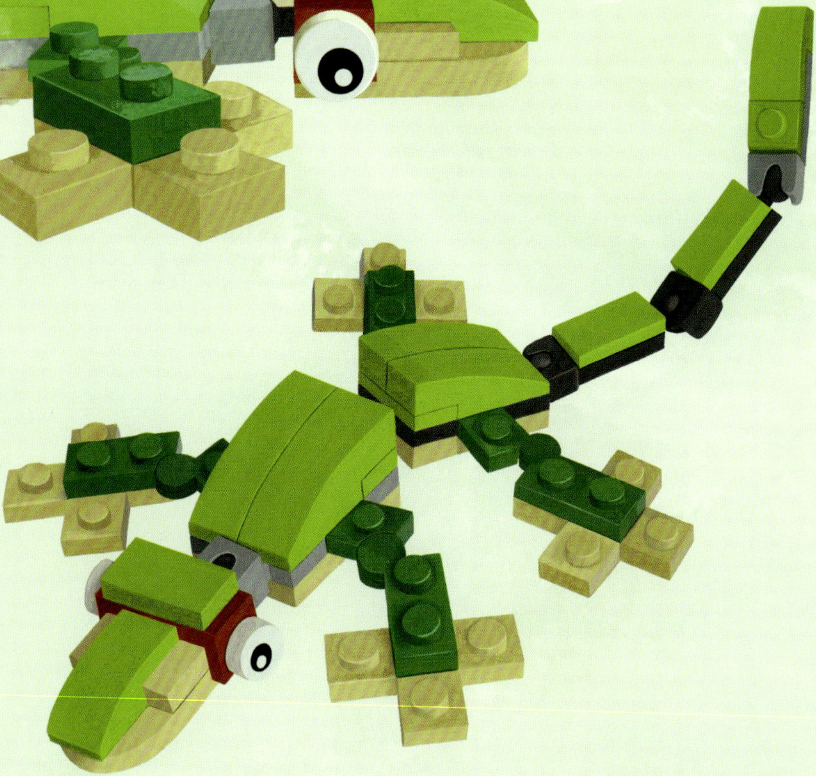

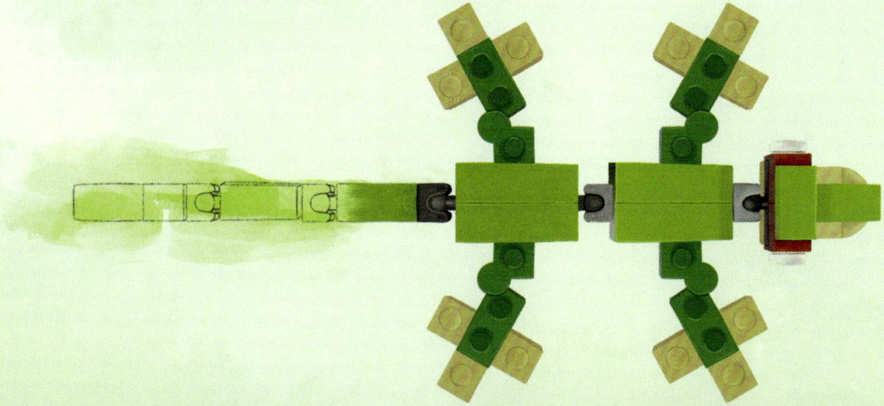

DAY GECKO

Phelsuma madagascariensis

Primary Location: Madagascar and nearby islands
Primary Food Source: Insects, nectar, and fruit
Average Length: 4 to 10 in (10 to 25 cm)
Average Weight: 1.6 to 2.1 oz (45 to 60 g)

Day geckos are famous for their excellent climbing skills. They can walk up walls and across ceilings thanks to their lamellae, tiny plate-like structures on their feet covered in tiny hairlike structures that act as microscopic hooks, creating adhesion to surfaces. Day geckos are also well known for their large, striking eyes and their long tails, which are at least as long as their bodies!

- *Day geckos don't have eyelids. Instead, they have small plates over their eyes! That's why they're always licking their eyes—it's how they keep those plates clean and moist.*
- *The day gecko's bright-green coloring helps these reptiles camouflage themselves in tropical environments.*
- *Day geckos can make all sorts of noises: barks, croaks, squeaks, and clicks. In fact, they're the only lizard with such a wide range of vocalizations—most other lizards only hiss or make simple sounds.*

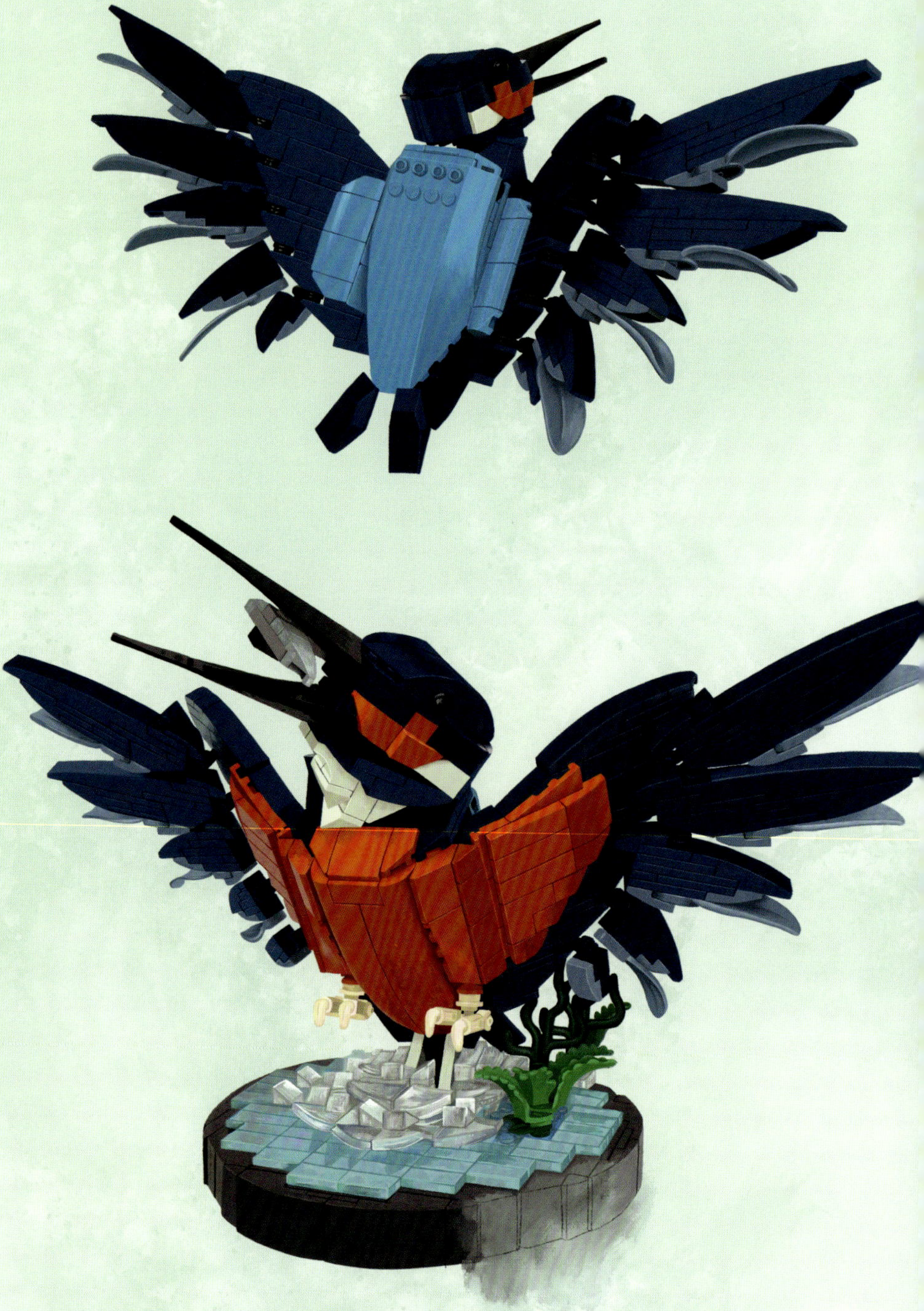

COMMON KINGFISHER

Alcedo atthis

Primary Location: Europe, Asia, and North Africa
Primary Food Source: Fish and aquatic invertebrates
Average Length: 6.3 to 6.7 in (16 to 17 cm)
Average Weight: 0.9 to 1.4 oz (26 to 39 g)

Kingfishers are mostly solitary animals—until it comes time to nest in the spring! They build their nests by finding a water source, then burrowing into a nearby bank. These burrows are usually more than 2 ft long. Both the male and female kingfishers are responsible for caring for the young when they are first born, although only the female tends to the chicks at night.

- *Kingfishers have a transparent third eyelid that allows them to see both in the air and in the water.*
- *Can you guess how kingfishers eat, based on their name? They fish! Kingfishers dive into the water to grab prey with their sharp beaks.*

COMMON KINGFISHER

Alcedo atthis

BONUS INFO AND FUN FACTS!

Common kingfishers are picky eaters—both in terms of their diet (99 percent of which is fish) and also in terms of *how* they eat their prey, which is very specific! Every time kingfishers grab a fish, they follow the same routine before eating it: First, they grip the fish by its tail and hit the fish against their perch. Then they shift the fish lengthwise and swallow it headfirst.

- *Unlike many other birds, kingfishers are not known for being great singers. Instead, they communicate in sharp whistling sounds.*
- *According to one famous French myth, the kingfisher got its beautiful coloring when it flew over the sun to avoid a storm. Once it was high in the air, the sky turned the kingfisher's back blue, and the sun turned its belly yellow!*

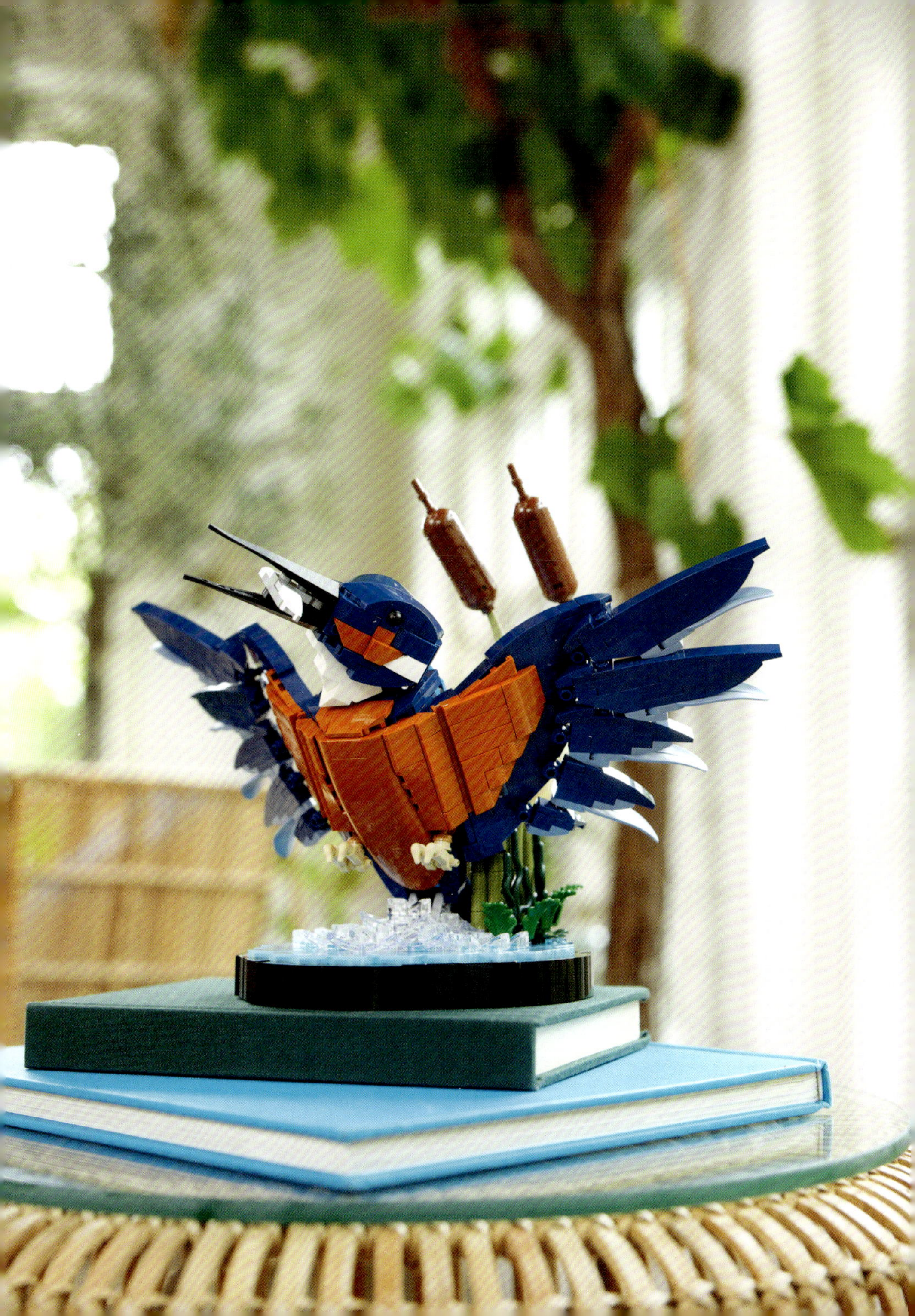

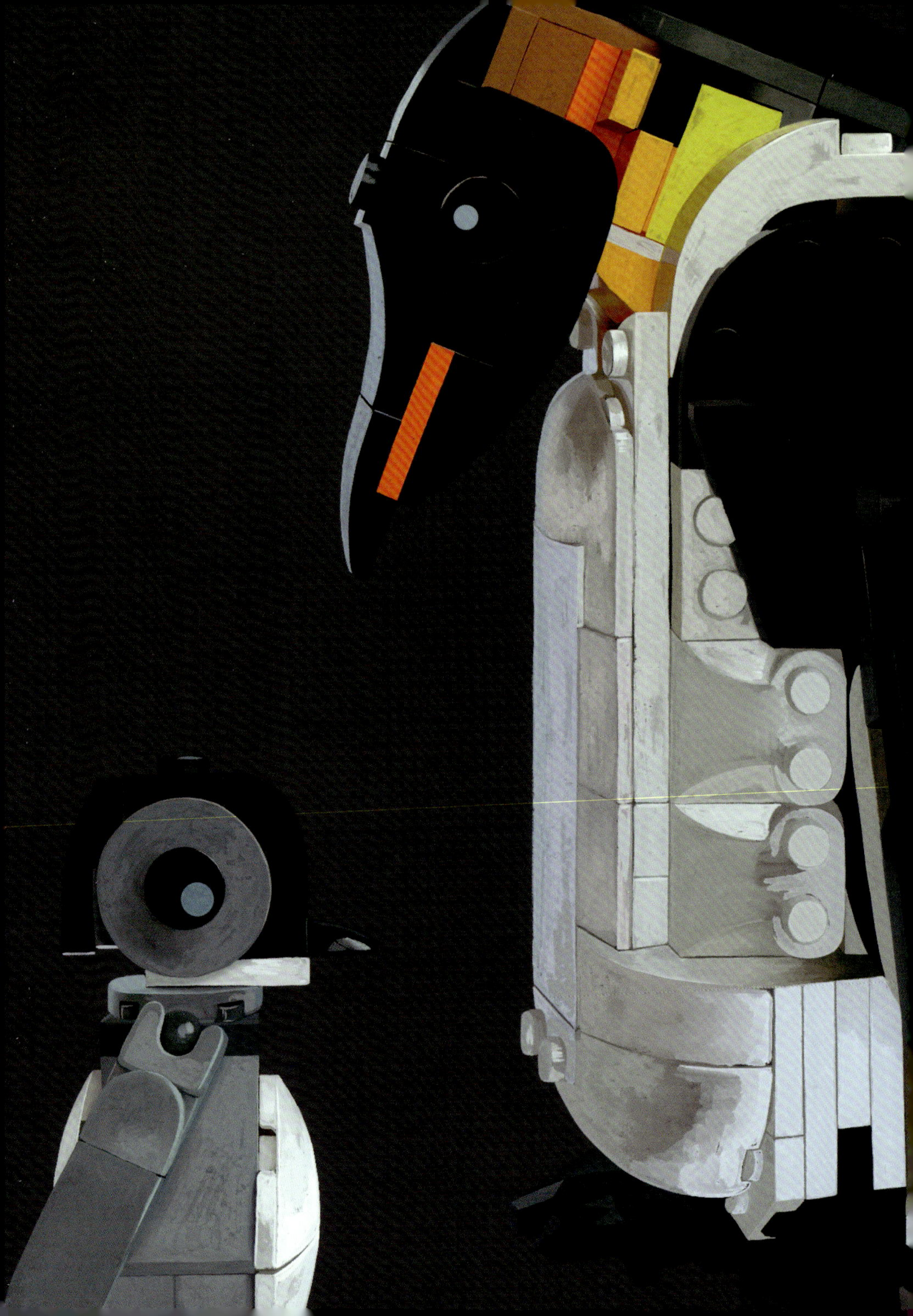

Near Water: From Wetlands to the Arctic

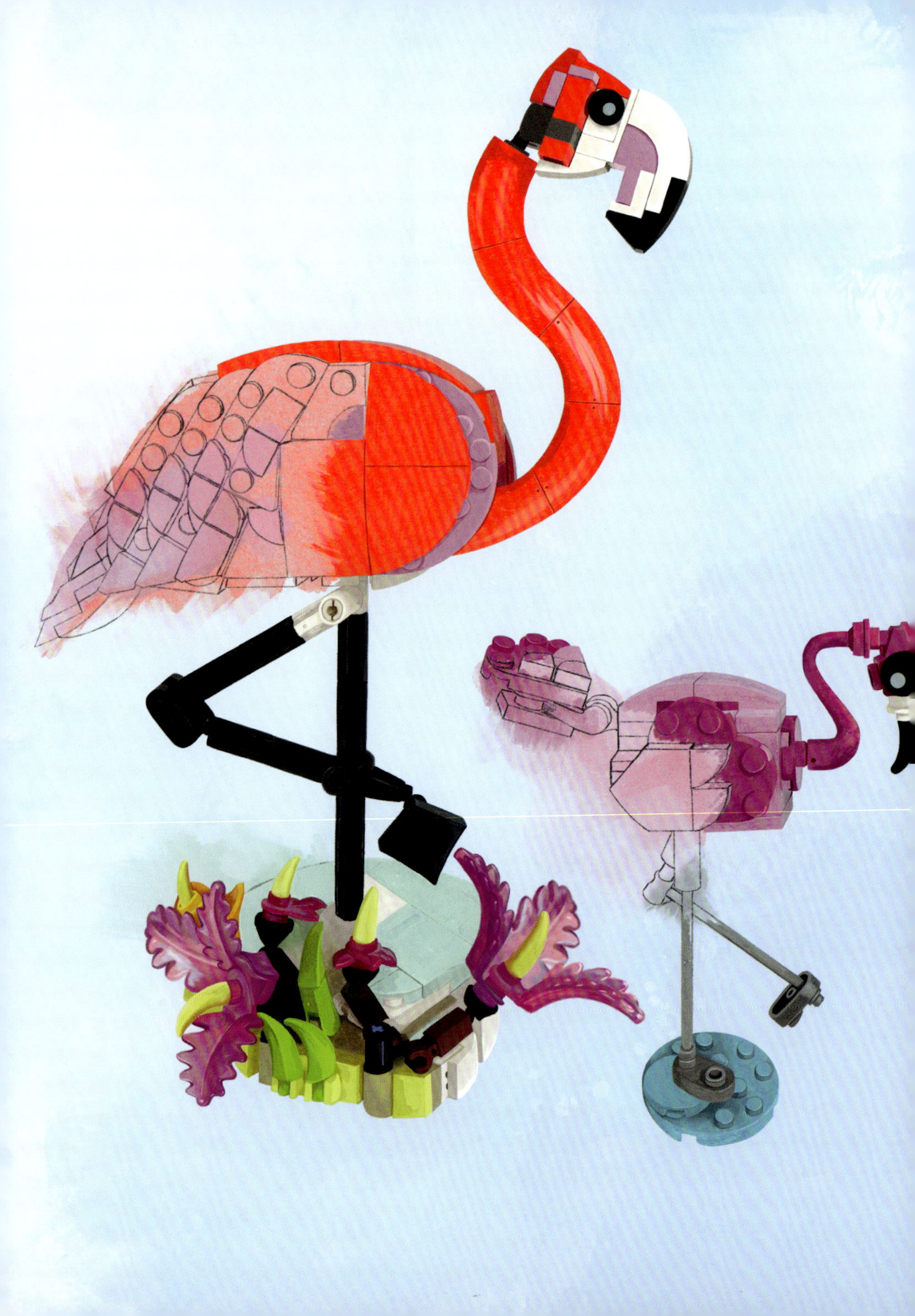

FLAMINGO

Phoenicopterus ruber

Primary Location: West Indies, northern South America, and the Yucatán Peninsula
Primary Food Source: Algae, small crustaceans, diatoms, and aquatic invertebrates
Average Length: 47 to 57 in (120 to 145 cm)
Average Weight: 4.6 to 9 lb (2.1 to 4.1 kg)

The flamingo species *Phoenicopterus ruber* is often called the American flamingo. These flamingos are highly social and sometimes live in colonies that include thousands of flamingos. A group of flamingos, somewhat aptly, is often referred to as a *flamboyance*. Both male and female flamingos take care of their young—and both supply their offspring with crop milk secretions from their own bodies.

- *When flamingos walk, it looks like their legs are bending backward! This is because the middle joint on their legs is their ankle, not their knee. Their knee is much higher up the leg, near their body.*
- *Flamingos feed upside down! They stick their bills into salt water and then filter the mud and silt out of their food.*
- *Flamingos are great flyers. Once a pair of African flamingos made a great escape from a zoo in Wichita, Kansas, by taking off into the air. One of them was spotted 14 years later . . . all the way in Texas!*

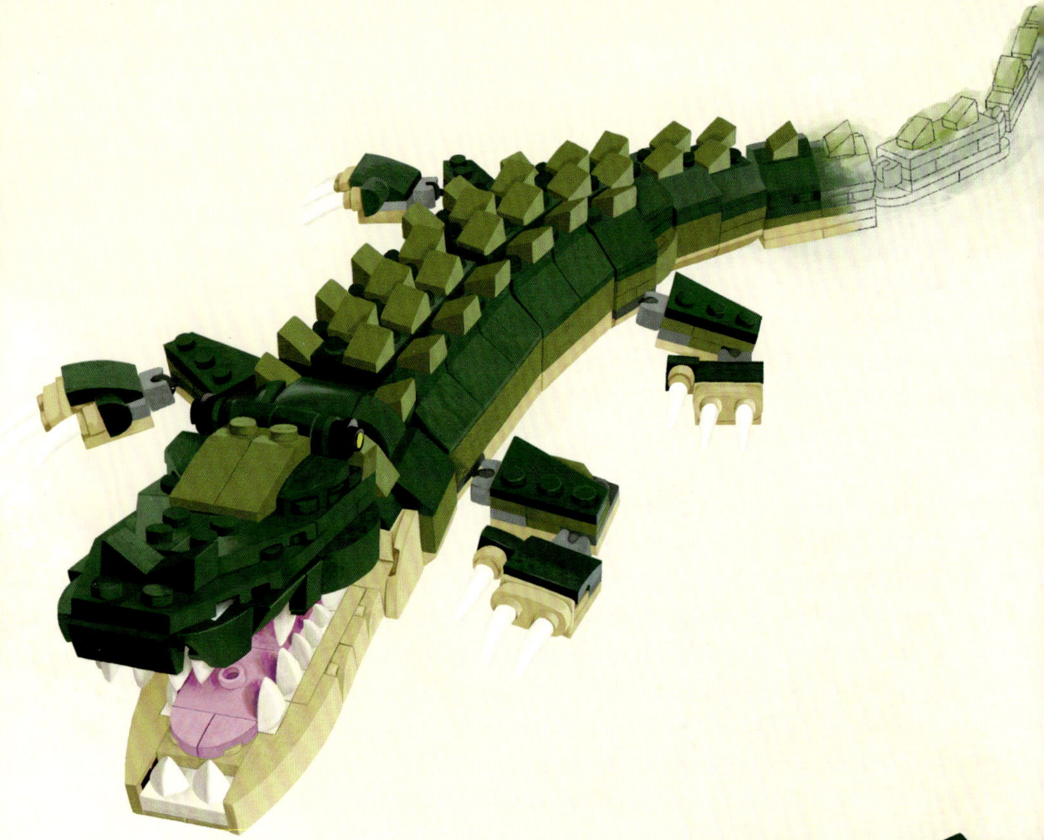

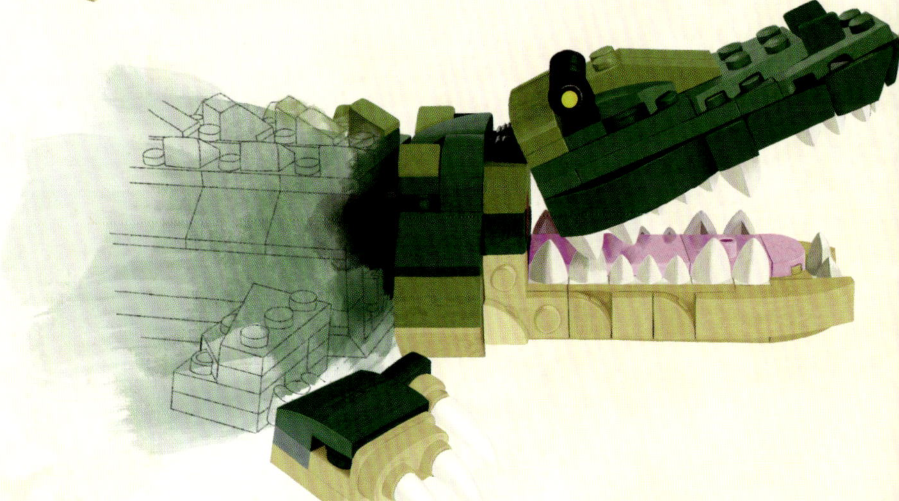

NILE CROCODILE

Crocodylus niloticus

Primary Location: Sub-Saharan Africa
Primary Food Source: Fish, mammals, birds, and other reptiles
Average Length: 9.8 to 16.4 ft (3 to 5 m)
Average Weight: 500 to 1,650 lb (225 to 750 kg)

Nile crocodiles are one of the largest reptiles in the world and among the most powerful predators in Africa. They have a bite force measuring 22 kN (kilonewtons), which means that when they clamp their jaws shut, the pressure is about the same as a car pressing down on a single point! These reptiles are wily predators, thanks to the placement of their nostrils, eyes, and ears on the tops of their heads. This allows them to fully submerge their bodies underwater while still having use of their senses. Crocodiles are ambush predators, which means that they can wait a long time—sometimes even weeks—for the exact right moment to attack their prey.

- *How can you tell the difference between a crocodile and an alligator? Crocodiles have longer, narrower heads and V-shaped snouts, while alligators have broad, U-shaped snouts. It's important to know the difference—crocodiles are much more aggressive than alligators!*
- *There is a Nile crocodile in Kenya that is 15 ft (4.6 m) long and weighs 2,200 lb (1,000 kg)!*

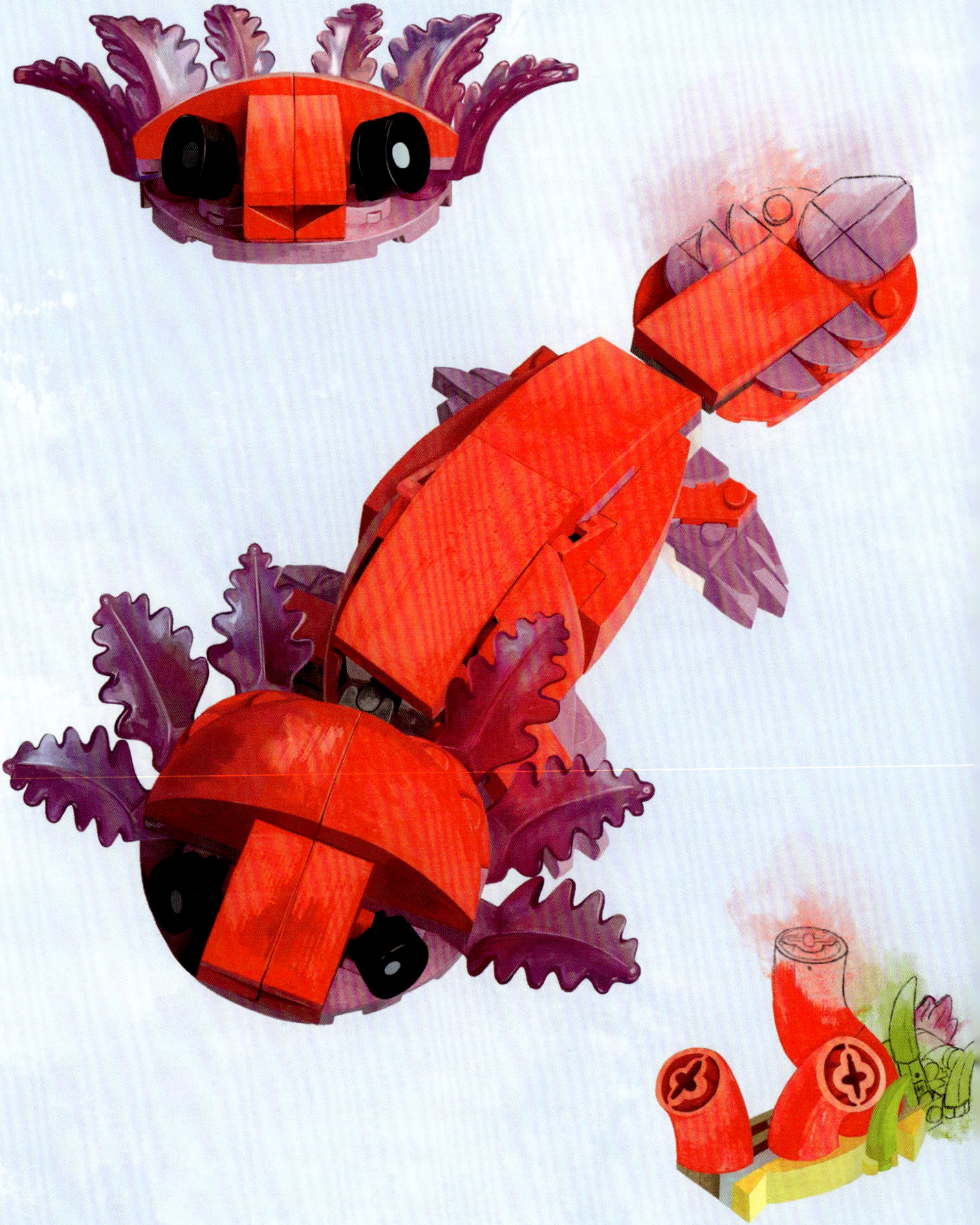

AXOLOTL

Ambystoma mexicanum

Primary Location: Valley of Mexico
Primary Food Source: Worms, small fish, insects, mollusks, and crustaceans
Average Length: 6 to 12 in (15 to 30 cm)
Average Weight: 1.7 to 7 oz (50 to 200 g)

The name *axolotl* comes from the Aztec god Xolotl, which can translate to "water monster" in Nahuatl. Axolotls feature heavily in Mexican culture and even appear on Mexico's 50-peso bill. They once lived in many interconnected freshwater lakes and canals in the Mexican wetlands, but today they are only found in Lake Xochimilco. Axolotls are considered critically endangered, and it's estimated that there are only about 50 to 1,000 adult axolotls left in the wild.

- *Like something out of a sci-fi novel, axolotls can regenerate their limbs, their gills, and even parts of their eyes, hearts, and brains!*
- *Forever young! Axolotls hold on to their larval characteristics, even into adulthood. While other amphibians eventually lose their gills to survive on land, axolotls keep theirs forever and stay in the water for their whole lives.*
- *Axolotls have one of the largest known animal genomes! Some estimates say their genomes are 10 times larger than that of a human.*

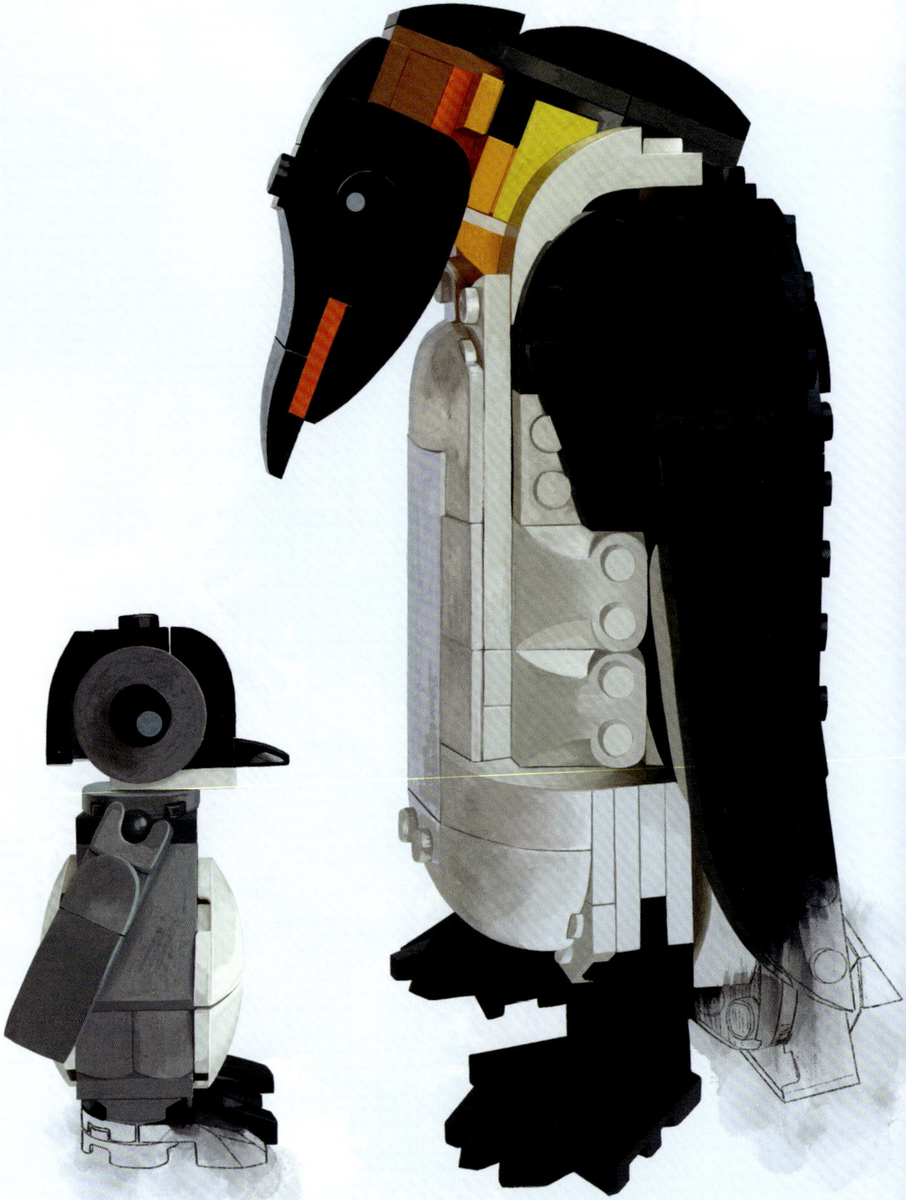

EMPEROR PENGUIN

Aptenodytes forsteri

Primary Location: Antarctic sea ice and surrounding waters
Primary Food Source: Fish, squid, and krill
Average Length: 39 to 47 in (100 to 120 cm)
Average Weight: 49 to 99 lb (22 to 45 kg)

Emperor penguins are the largest penguin species alive today. They live in extremely cold areas, where temperatures can drop as low as –58°F (–50°C) and winds can get as high as 124 mph (200 kph). They have developed a good deal of insulation in order to survive these conditions, including fat reserves that are up to 1.2 in (3 cm) thick and two layers of feathers. These feathers resemble scales and reportedly don't ruffle until winds reach as high as 68 mph (110 kph).

- *There was once a penguin that was three times the size of the emperor penguin! This penguin lived around 56 to 60 million years ago and weighed approximately 350 lb (160 kg). Its generic name, Kumimanu, comes from the Māori language and means "monster bird."*
- *The longest dive ever recorded for an emperor penguin is 1,850 ft (564 m). That's about the same height as one and a half Eiffel Towers!*

EMPEROR PENGUIN

Aptenodytes forsteri

BONUS INFO AND FUN FACTS!

Emperor penguins' feet contain special fats to keep them warm as they stand on the freezing ice, and they have strong claws that allow them to grip the ice without falling. They also keep warm by huddling together in large groups. The penguins take turns standing on the outside of the group so that no single penguin is exposed to the harsh conditions for too long. Once a penguin has warmed up inside the huddle, they'll move to the outside so that other penguins can take a turn getting warm.

- *Male emperor penguins incubate their eggs by balancing them on their feet. They have a pouch that folds down over the egg to protect it from the cold.*
- *It takes 65 to 75 days for an emperor penguin's egg to hatch. During all that time, the male penguins don't eat anything!*

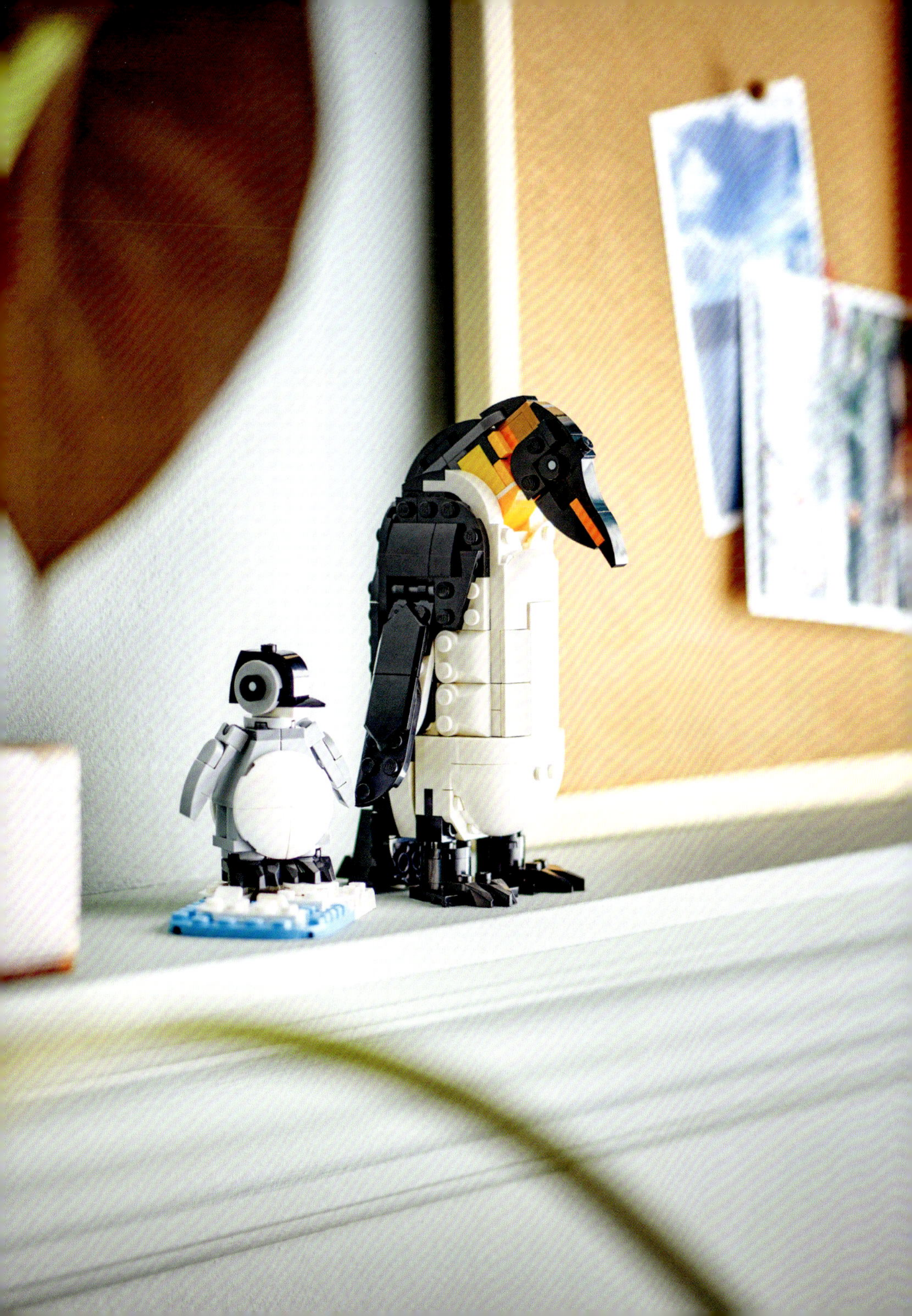

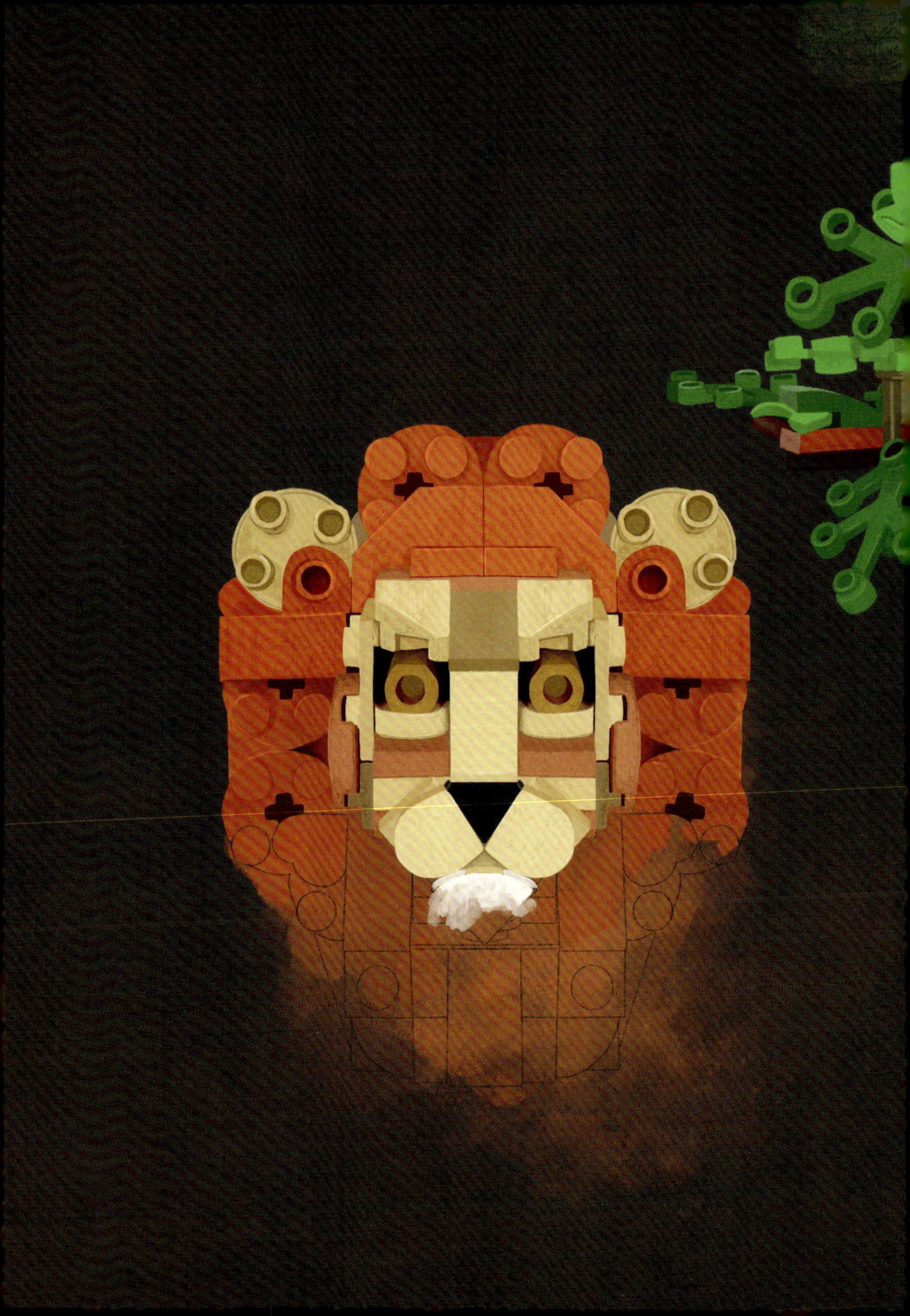

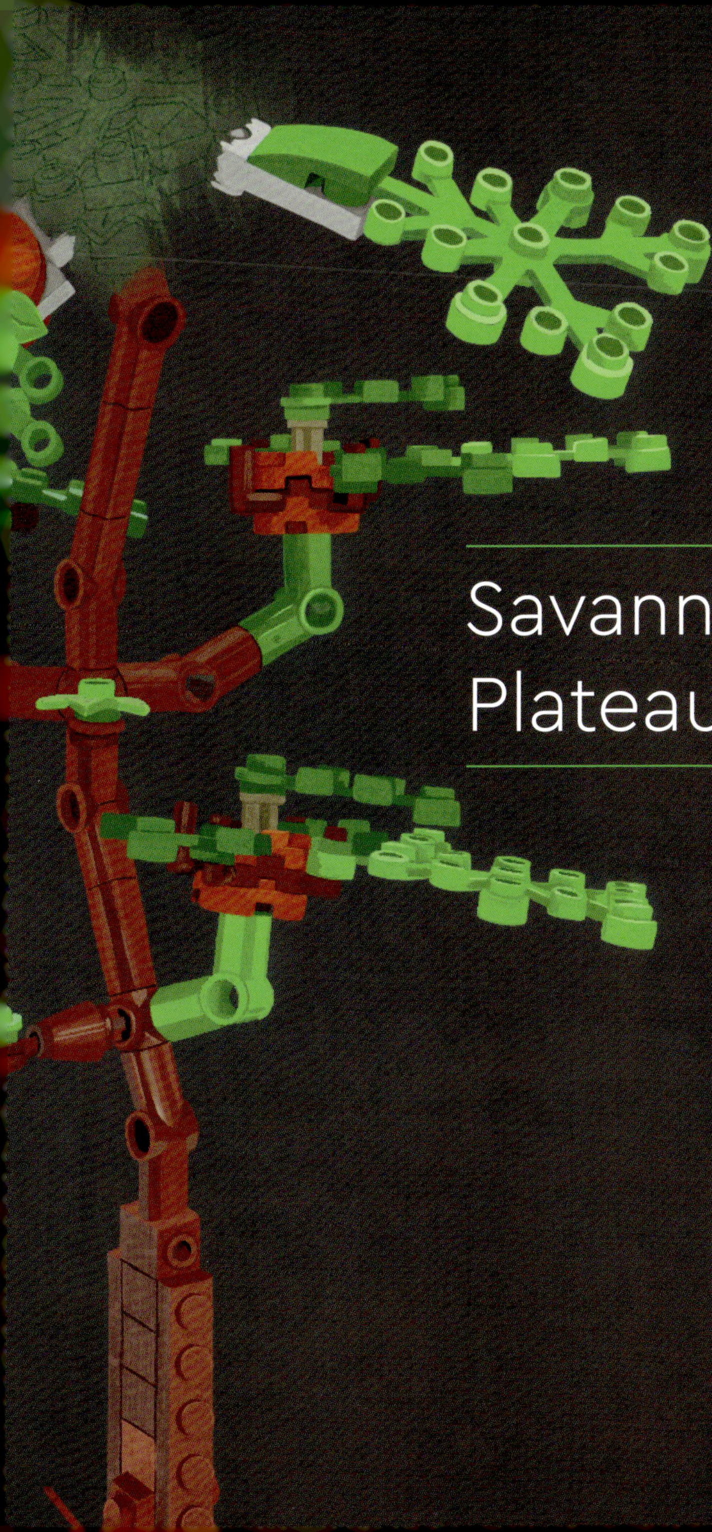

Savannas and Plateaus

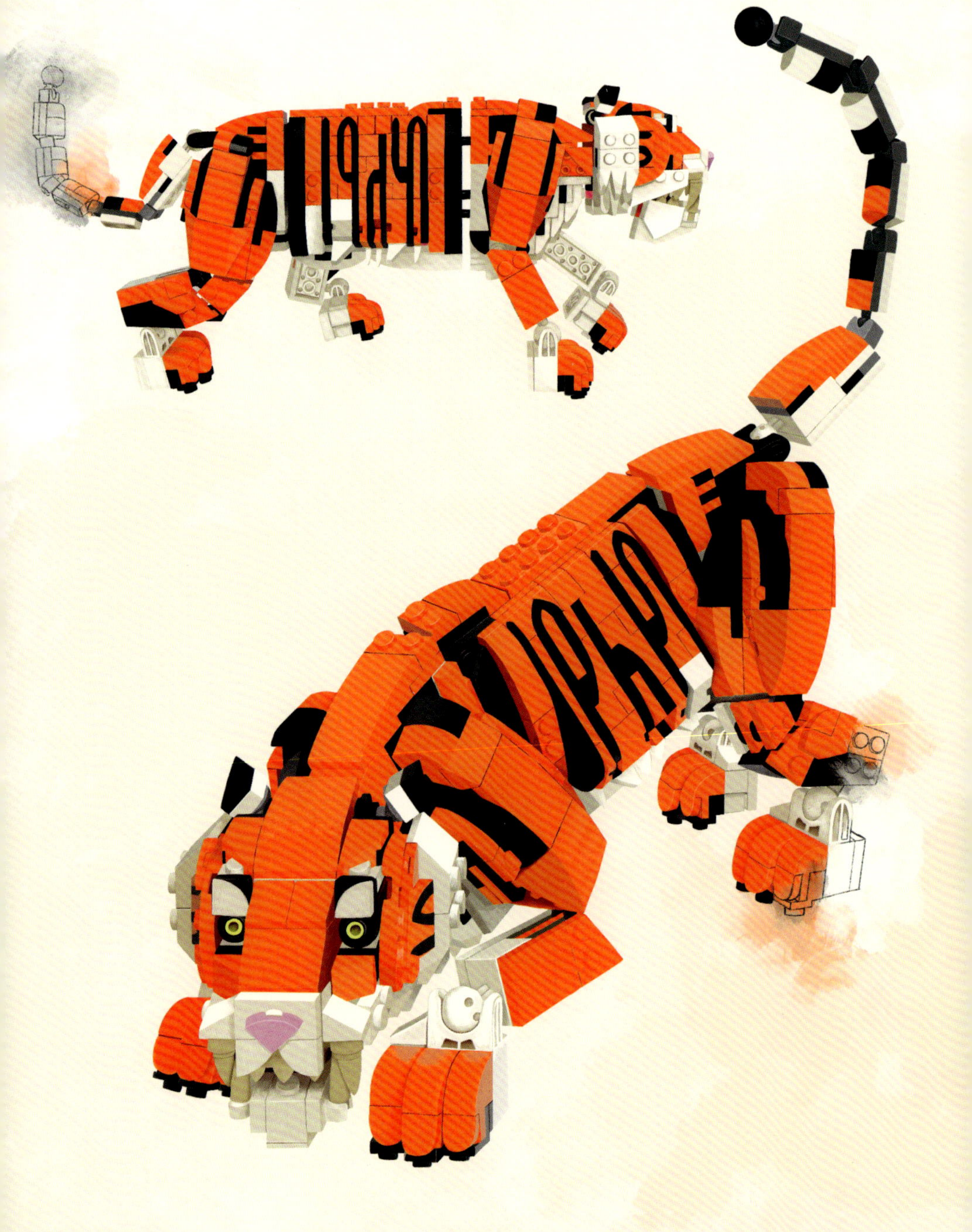

BENGAL TIGER

Panthera tigris tigris

Primary Location: India, Bangladesh, Nepal, Bhutan, and Myanmar
Primary Food Source: Large ungulates, such as deer and wild boar
Average Length: Up to 10.5 ft (3.2 m)
Average Weight: Up to 650 lb (295 kg)

The Bengal tiger is the national animal of both India and Bangladesh. Bengal tigers are the most common tiger species, making up about half of all tigers in the wild. As recently as the early 1900s, there were an estimated 100,000 tigers in India. By the early 2000s, that number had diminished significantly—to around 1,400 remaining. Today, Bengal tigers are considered endangered. They are also nocturnal and use their striped coats for camouflage. Each tiger's pattern of stripes is unique—like fingerprints!

- *Tigers have pads on their feet—like little socks—to prevent them from making noise while hunting.*
- *Tigers have a lot to say! They are known to make a wide range of sounds—from grunting to growling to hissing—and researchers believe that each sound means something different.*
- *Tigers will cover their food with dirt and leaves to hide it from other predators. They don't like to share!*

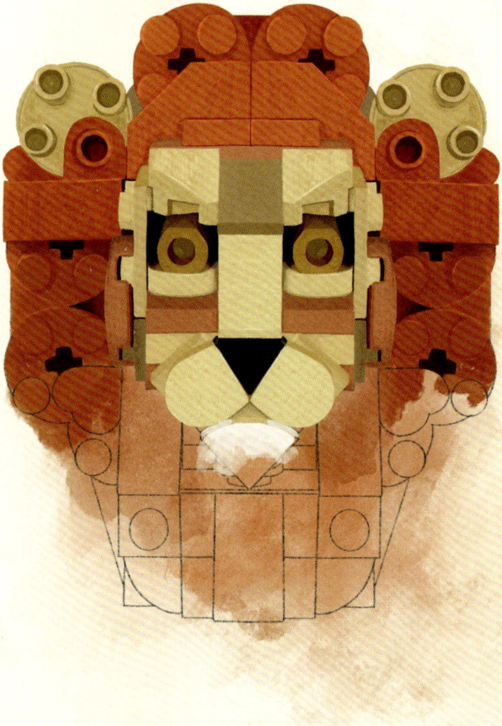

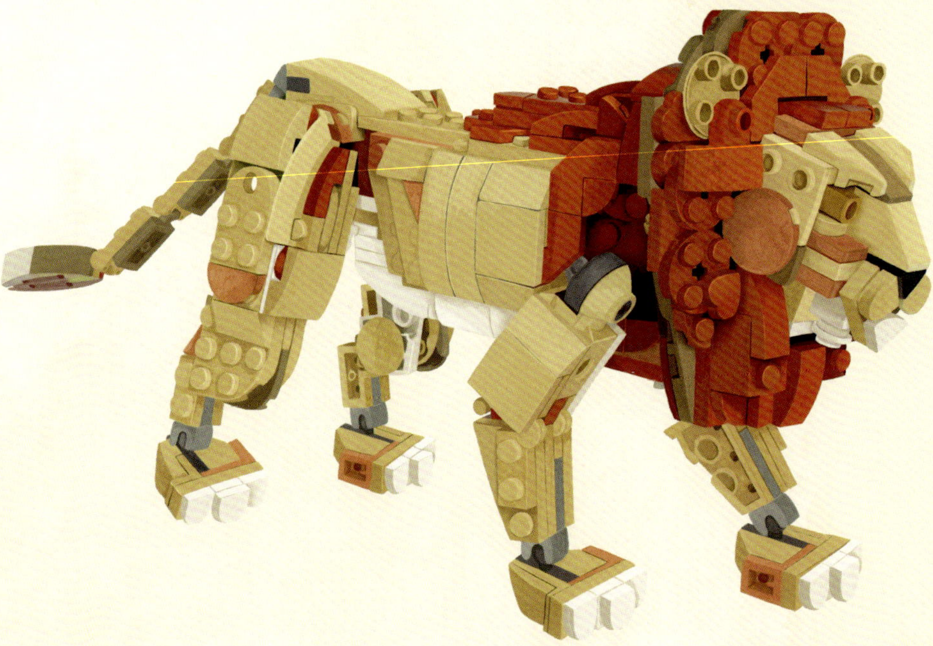

LION

Panthera leo

Primary Location: Sub-Saharan Africa
Primary Food Source: Large herbivores, like zebras, wildebeests, and buffalo
Average Length: 7 to 10 ft (210 to 300 cm)
Average Weight: 270 to 570 lb (120 to 260 kg)

Lions have been a symbol of strength and power across the globe for centuries. They're the most social of all wild cats and move in groups called prides, usually made up of around 15 lions. Lions take care of one another and are often seen rubbing heads or licking each other. All male lions leave their pride at some point, while lionesses usually stay in the prides where they were born. Only male lions have manes, and their colors vary significantly based on different factors, including the lion's fitness. Darker manes signify strength and tend to predict a longer tenure for the lion inside a pride.

- *Every day is a lazy Sunday for the lion! Lions spend the vast majority of their time—around 20 hours a day—relaxing.*
- *Everyone has a role to play! Male lions usually focus on territory defense, while lionesses focus on hunting. During group hunts, each lioness has her own special position.*

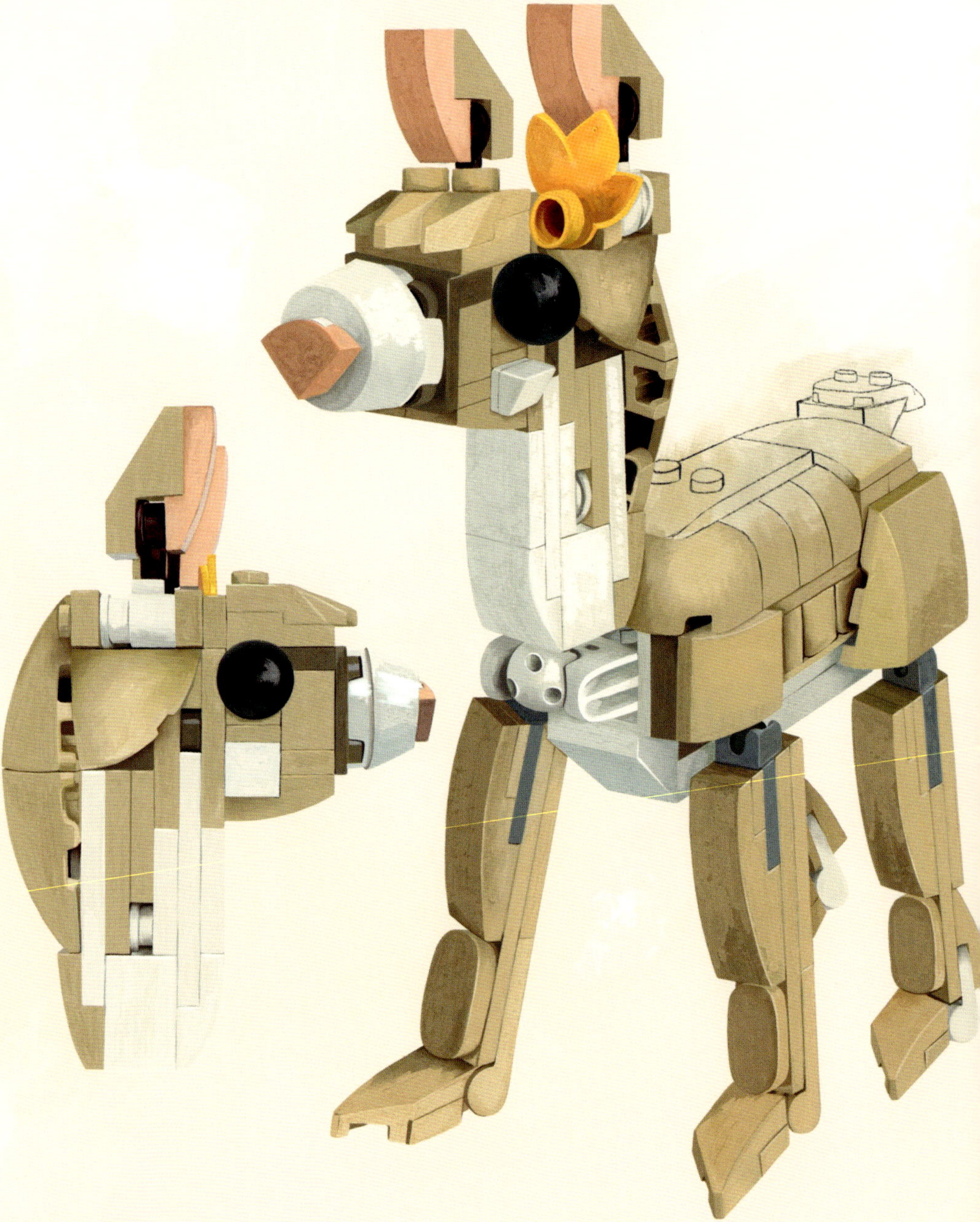

LLAMA

Lama glama

Primary Location: Andes Mountains
Primary Food Source: Grasses, shrubs, and other low-protein, high-fiber plants
Average Length: 5.5 to 6 ft (1.7 to 1.8 m)
Average Weight: 280 to 450 lb (130 to 200 kg)

Llamas have been domesticated for over 6,000 years, trained primarily by Andean cultures to transport goods. They're great with people—friendly and gentle—and they're fast learners, able to watch another llama or a human do a task only a handful of times before they can replicate it themselves. But when people overhandle young llamas, it can actually make them more difficult to control when they get older. They start to view humans as part of their herd and try to assert dominance over them. This problem is so prevalent that it has its own name—berserk llama syndrome!

- *Llamas assert dominance—and even admonish lower-ranking llamas—by spitting!*
- *You can tell how a llama is feeling based on the makeup of their saliva! They have three stomach compartments, and depending on how upset they're feeling, they will reach farther back into those compartments to draw up their saliva.*

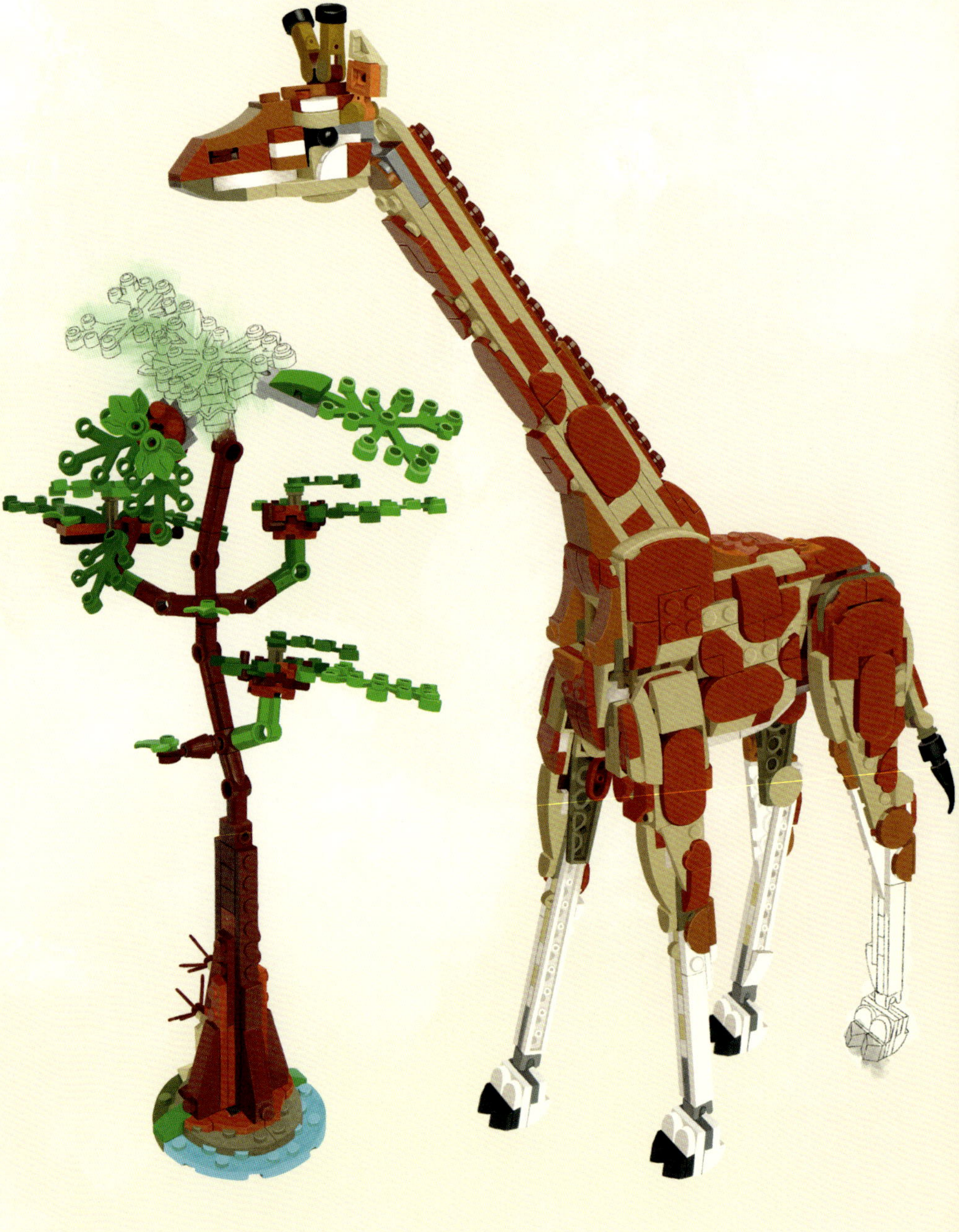

GIRAFFE

Giraffa camelopardalis

Primary Location: Sub-Saharan Africa
Primary Food Source: Leaves, especially from acacia trees
Average Height: 14 to 19 ft (4.3 to 5.7 m)
Average Weight: 1,760 to 2,645 lb (800 to 1,200 kg)

The giraffe is the tallest land animal on earth. Giraffes' necks are famously long, but they actually have only seven vertebrae, just like most other mammals (including humans). Their vertebrae are just *longer*. But it wasn't always this way. Ancestors of giraffes had short necks, and it's still not known exactly why their necks evolved to be so long. Scientists have a few different theories. Perhaps their long necks evolved to help male giraffes show dominance or so they could spot predators from afar.

- *Male giraffes love to swing their necks at one another, trying to show dominance by knocking their rivals off-balance. These matches can last for more than half an hour, and the giraffe who stays the most upright wins!*
- *Giraffes have black tongues! Do you know why? Scientists think it may help protect their tongues from sunburn.*

GIRAFFE

Giraffa camelopardalis

BONUS INFO AND FUN FACTS!

Giraffes move in small groups that are usually made up of all-female giraffes or all-male giraffes, but they still make time to mingle. Their groups socialize with one another frequently, and they are not particularly territorial. In fact, scientists have found that socializing has health benefits for giraffes: The more time a female giraffe spends with other giraffes, the longer she lives.

- *Talk about a power nap! Giraffes will sometimes sleep for as little as a minute or two at a time. In total, they need only 30 minutes to 2 hours of sleep per day.*
- *Giraffes don't need a lot of water to survive. They can go for days at a time without drinking.*
- *Giraffes may not look particularly nimble, but they are surprisingly fast and can reach speeds of about 35 mph!*
- *A giraffe's spots are like fingerprints in that no two giraffes have the same pattern. Each spot has a large blood vessel and sweat glands underneath it, which may help with thermoregulation.*

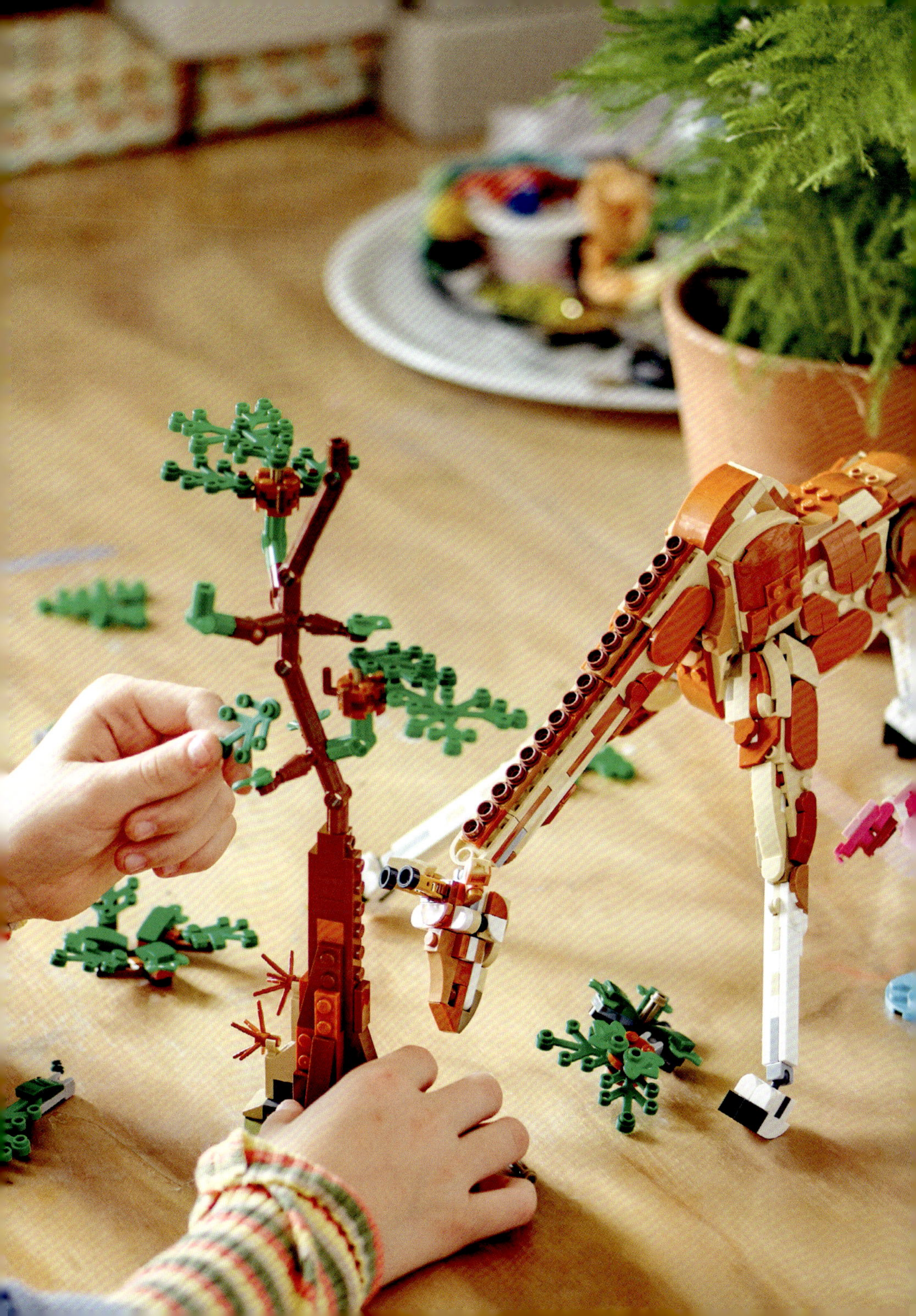

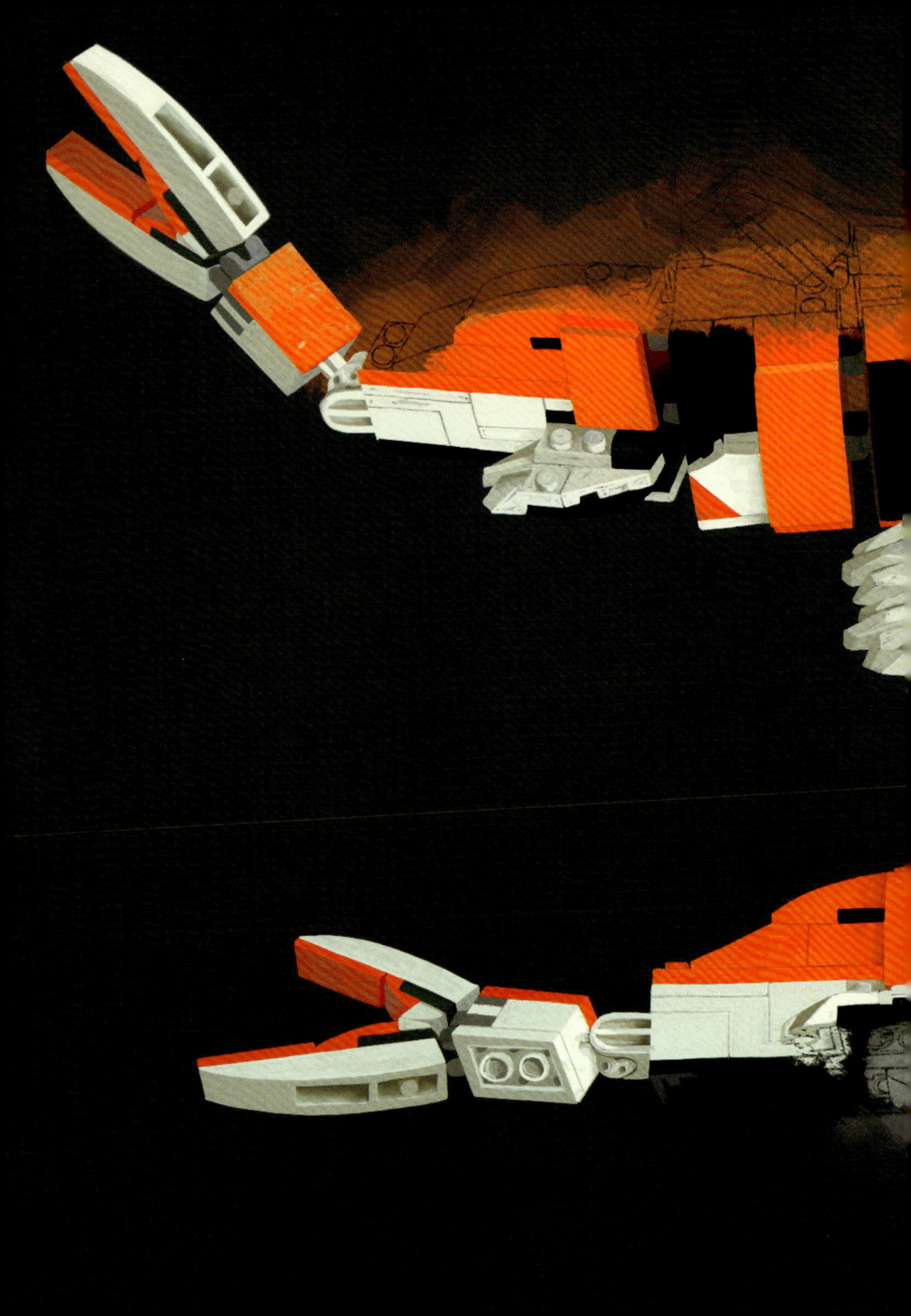

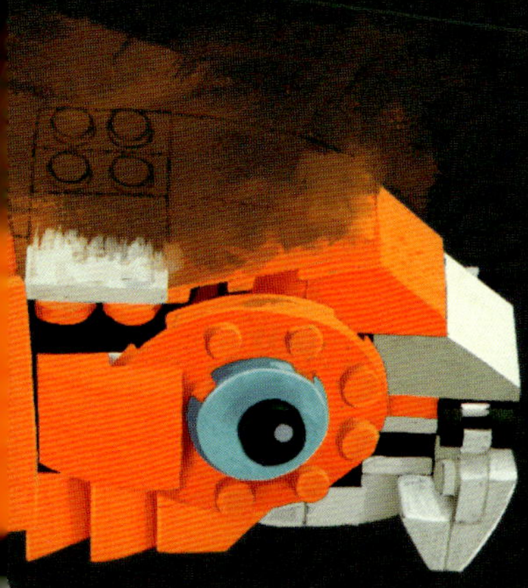

Underwater Animals

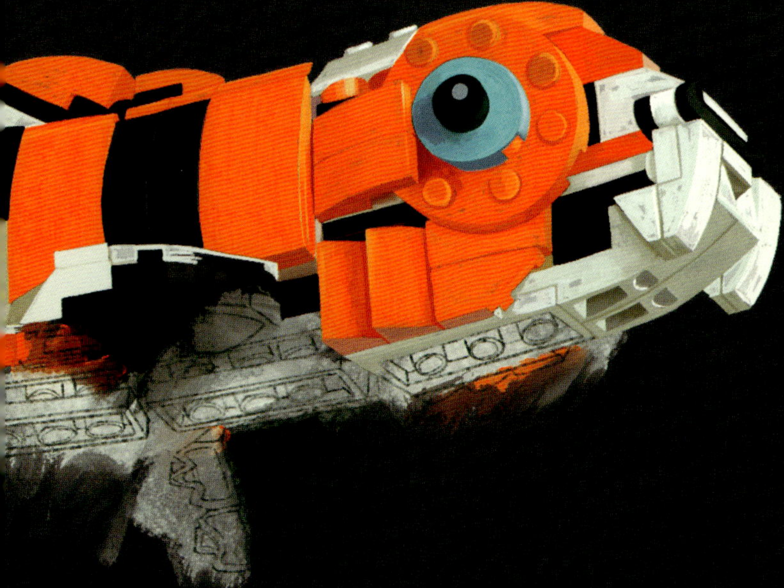

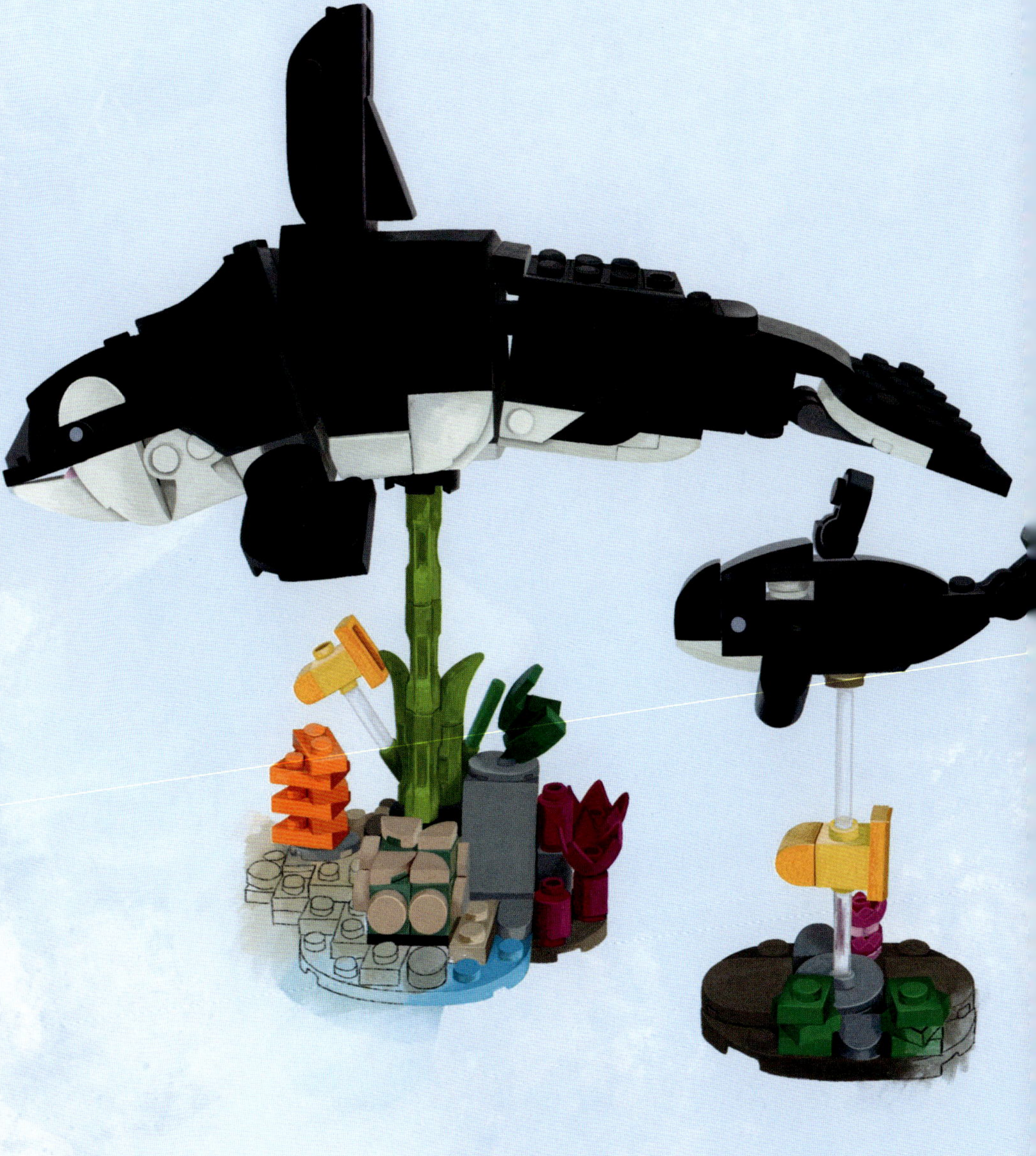

ORCA

Orcinus orca

Primary Location: All oceans worldwide
Primary Food Source: Varies by population, but includes fish, mammals, sea turtles, and seabirds
Average Length: 16 to 26 ft (5 to 8 m)
Average Weight: 3,000 to 12,000 lb (1,361 to 5,442 kg)

Orcas are apex predators and the largest members of the oceanic dolphin family. Their social structures are so complex that they rival those of elephants and higher primates. Orcas live in distinct populations that each have their own unique behaviors and diets. Within these populations, orcas travel in matrilineal family groups called pods. These pods are really tight-knit. They travel together for their whole lives, and orcas leave their pods for only a few hours at a time. In fact, there is only *one* instance ever recorded of an orca permanently separating from their pod!

- *Some female orcas live to be as old as 90, while male orcas tend not to live as long.*
- *Orcas have been caught playing with their food. People have spotted orcas wearing dead salmon on their heads—like hats! Scientists still don't know why they do this. Their best guess is that these orcas are just having fun.*
- *Some orcas need to consume as much as 325 lb (147 kg) of salmon a day. That's about the equivalent of a human eating 1,300 cheeseburgers!*

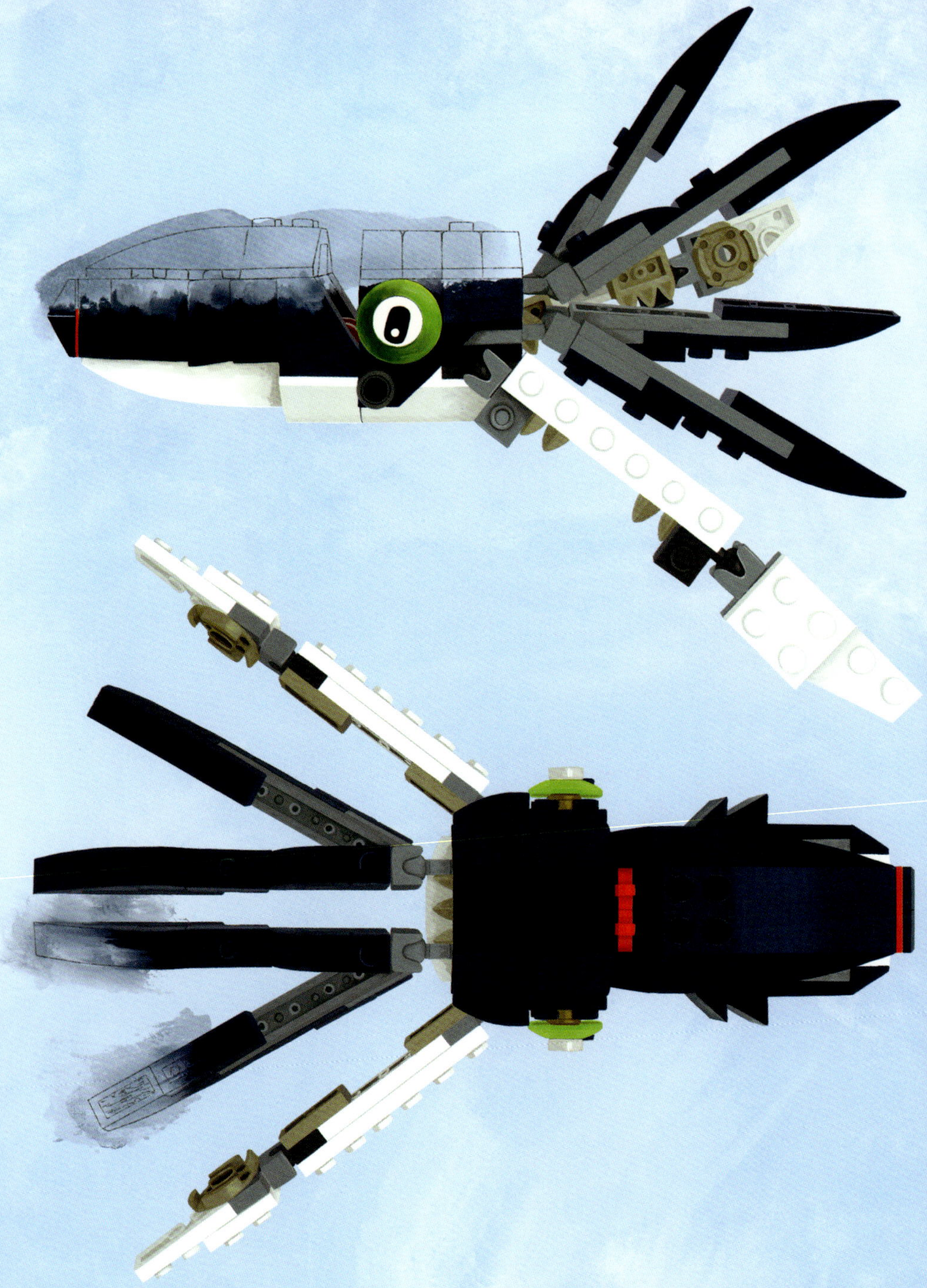

COMMON SQUID

Loligo vulgaris

Primary Location: Eastern Atlantic Ocean and Mediterranean Sea
Primary Food Source: Fish, crustaceans, and other cephalopods
Average Length: Up to 10 in (25 cm)
Average Weight: Up to 2.6 lb (1.2 kg)

Squid are a kind of cephalopod—from the Greek word for "head foot," in reference to how their heads are directly connected to their arms. The common squid has eight arms and two tentacles. They use their tentacles specifically to catch their prey. They have not one, not two, but *three* hearts! Two of the hearts deliver blood to the gills to gather more oxygen, while the third heart pumps that oxygenated blood to the rest of the body.

- *Cephalopods—which also include other sea creatures like octopuses and cuttlefish—are literally blue-blooded: Their blood is blue!*
- *Female common squid spawn up to 20,000 eggs at a time. Keep your eyes peeled if you end up on a beach after a big storm—sometimes those eggs wash up on shore!*
- *The common squid can change both its color and its texture! It will do this to blend into its surroundings, communicate with other squid, and attract potential mates.*

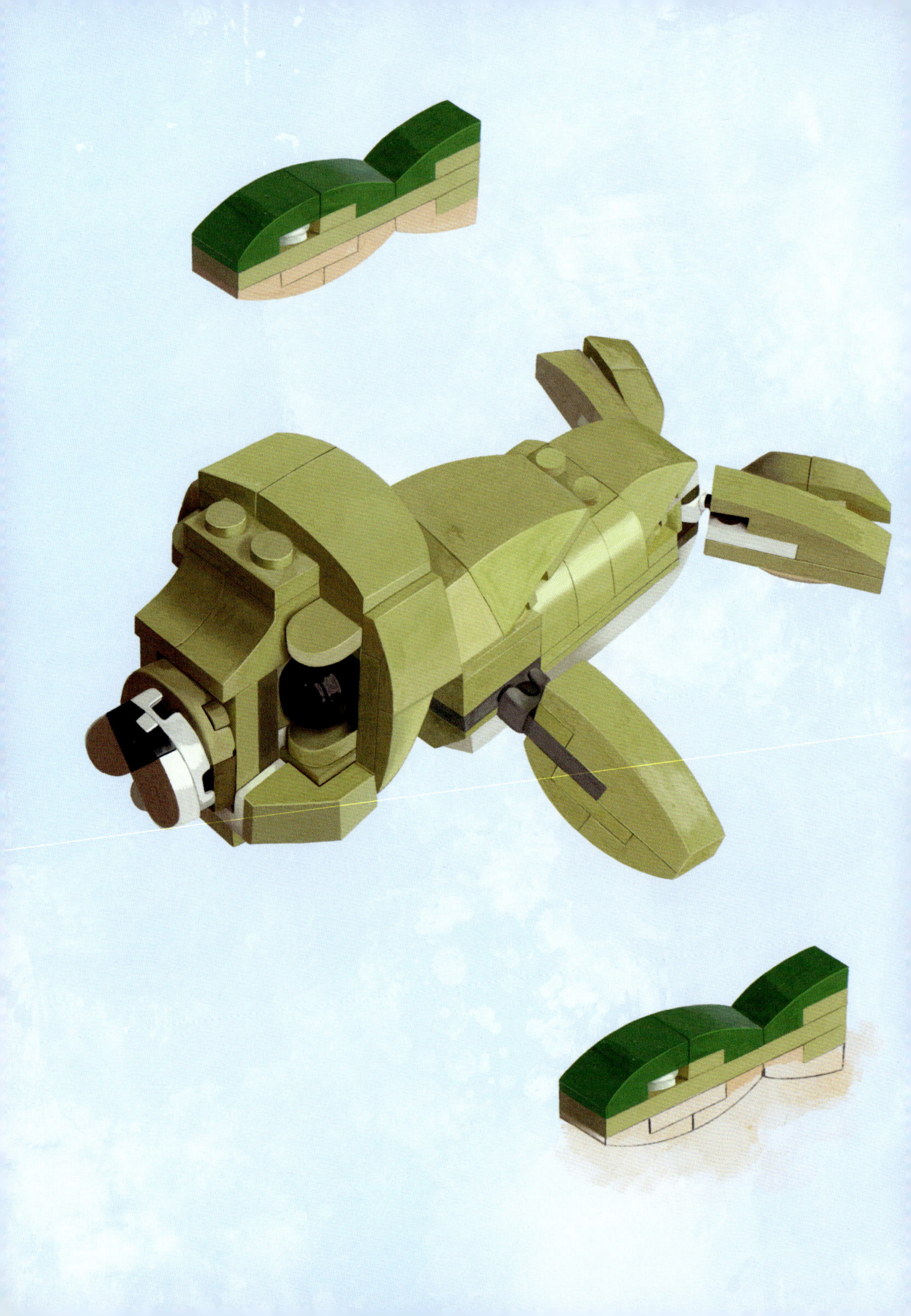

HARBOR SEAL

Phoca vitulina

Primary Location: Coastal waters of the Northern Hemisphere
Primary Food Source: Fish, squid, and crustaceans
Average Length: 4.3 to 6.6 ft (1.3 to 2 m)
Average Weight: 120 to 370 lb (55 to 170 kg)

Like all seals, harbor seals have evolved to be excellent swimmers. Their dives can reach up to 1,640 ft (500 m) deep, and they can stay underwater for up to 20 minutes at a time. It doesn't take them long to acquire these diving skills: Just hours after birth, harbor seal pups are ready to swim. Their senses are also heightened underwater compared to when they're out in the open air. They can hear better underwater and use their whiskers to find food and understand their surroundings.

- *Exactly how sensitive are harbor seals' whiskers? One study found that, using their whiskers, harbor seals could follow the wake of a miniature submarine—up to 30 seconds after it had already passed!*
- *A harbor seal named Hoover became famous for talking like a human! Believe it or not, he could say things like "Hello, there" and "Come over here"—in the same gruff voice as the man who raised him.*

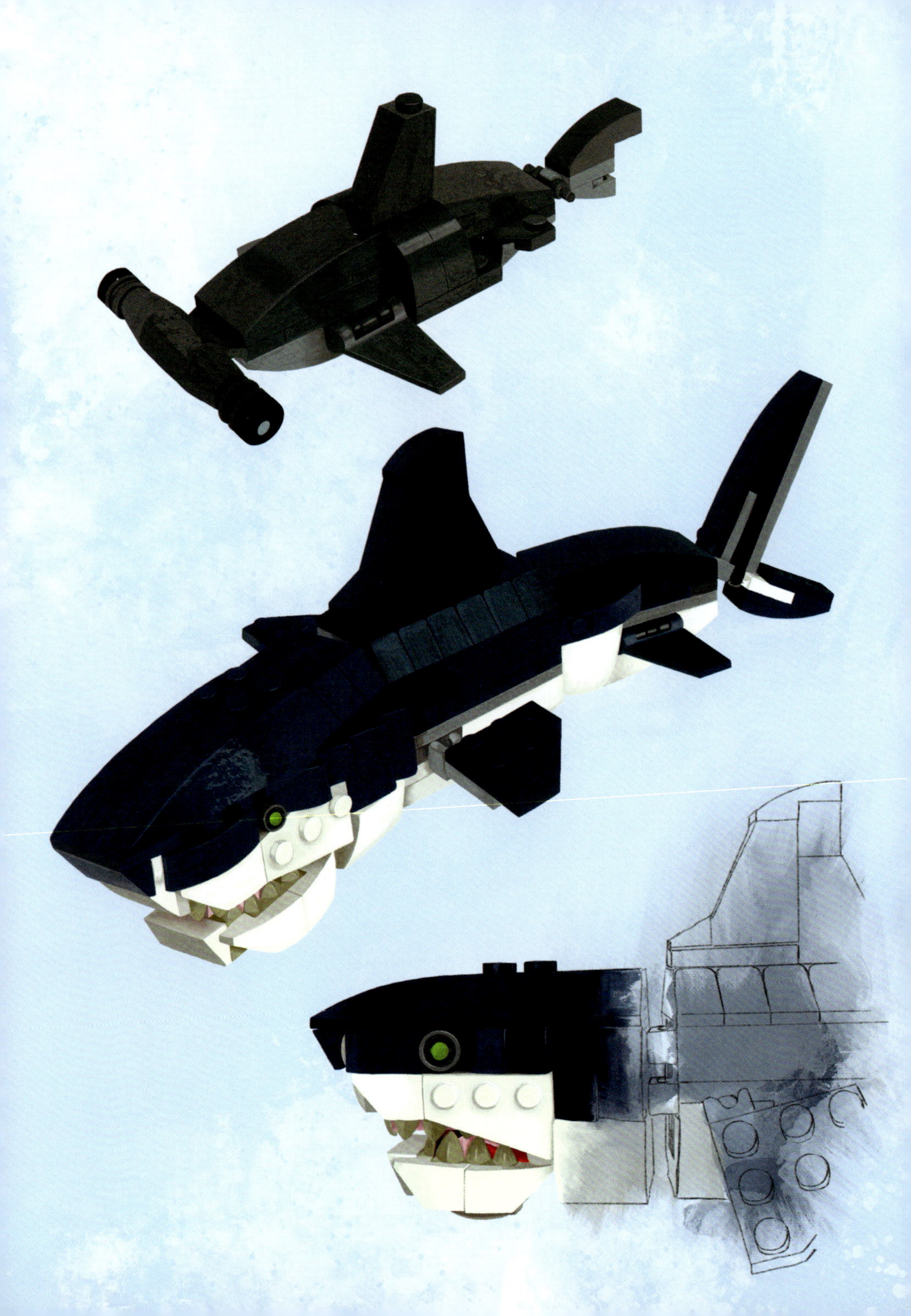

GREAT HAMMERHEAD

Sphyrna mokarran

Primary Location: Warm temperate and tropical coastal waters worldwide
Primary Food Source: Fish, squid, octopus, crustaceans, and other sharks
Average Length: 13.1 ft (4 m)
Average Weight: 500 lb (227 kg)

Hammerhead sharks are known for their particularly unusual shape. The placement of their eyes on the "hammer" part of their head is most likely in order to boost their vision—it allows them to see both above and below their bodies. You may think sharks are scary, but hammerheads are probably not as violent as you imagine: According to the International Shark Attack File, which collects data dating back to 1580, there have only been 17 reports of unprovoked attacks by hammerhead sharks, and none of those resulted in death.

GREAT WHITE SHARK

Carcharodon carcharias

Primary Location: Temperate and subtropical oceans worldwide
Primary Food Source: Marine mammals, fish, and seabirds
Average Length: 11 to 16 ft (3.4 to 4.9 m)
Average Weight: 1,500 to 5,000 lb (680 to 2,268 kg)

Sharks have been around much longer than dinosaurs—approximately 450 million years—and have survived five global mass extinctions. Great white sharks are the largest known predatory fish in the world. They have around 300 teeth, usually arranged in five or six rows. Today, the great white shark is classified as vulnerable across the world and as critically endangered in some parts of Europe and the Mediterranean.

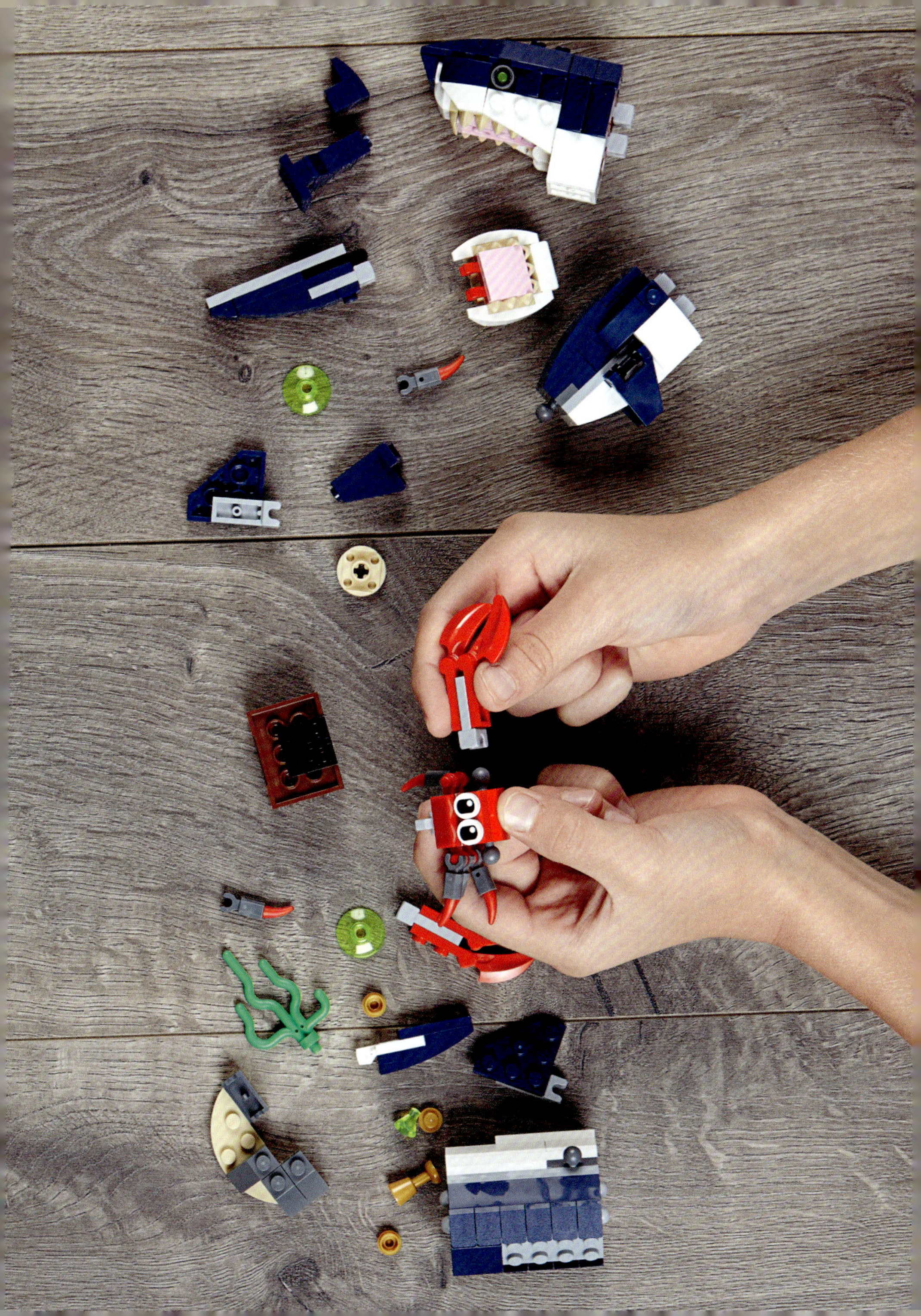

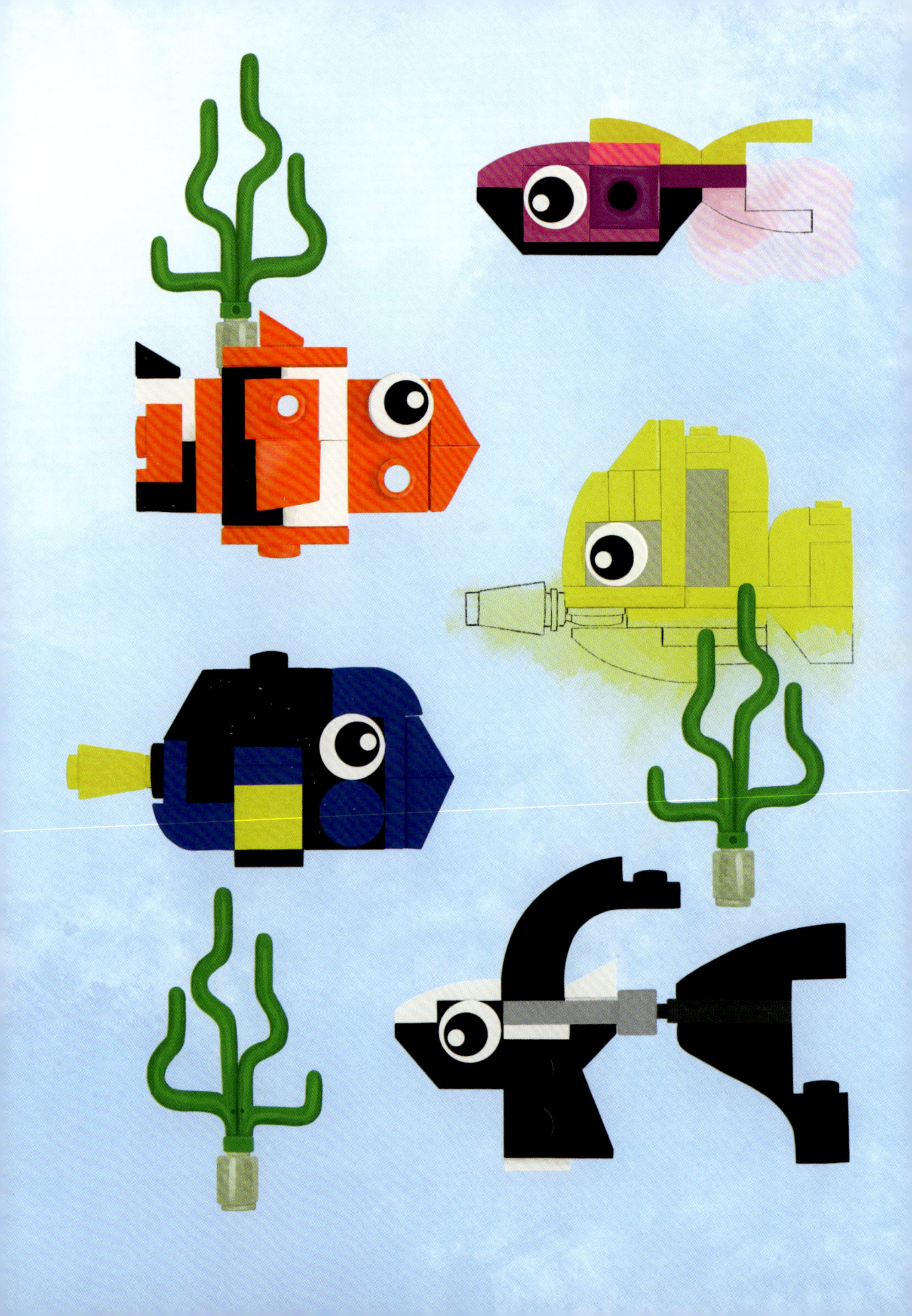

FISH OF THE CORAL REEF

ANTHIAS FISH, CLOWNFISH, YELLOW TANG, REGAL BLUE TANG, CARDINAL FISH

Coral reefs cover a tiny portion of the world's ocean surface area—less than 1 percent—but they are home to 25 percent of all marine fish species. It's estimated that over 4,000 species of fish live in coral reefs.

- *Anthias fish can change their sex from female to male in response to specific social cues.*
- *Clownfish live in sea anemones and have a special layer of mucus on their skin to protect them from the anemones' sting!*
- *Yellow tangs seem particularly attuned to the lunar cycle. They spawn year-round, but usually reproduction peaks around the full moon.*
- *This might come as a surprise, given their name, but regal blue tangs aren't always blue! They are born bright yellow and can change color—for example, when they become stressed, they may turn violet.*
- *After the female cardinal fish spawns eggs, the male cardinal fish holds on to these eggs for 20 days until they hatch—in his mouth! During this time, he does not eat anything.*

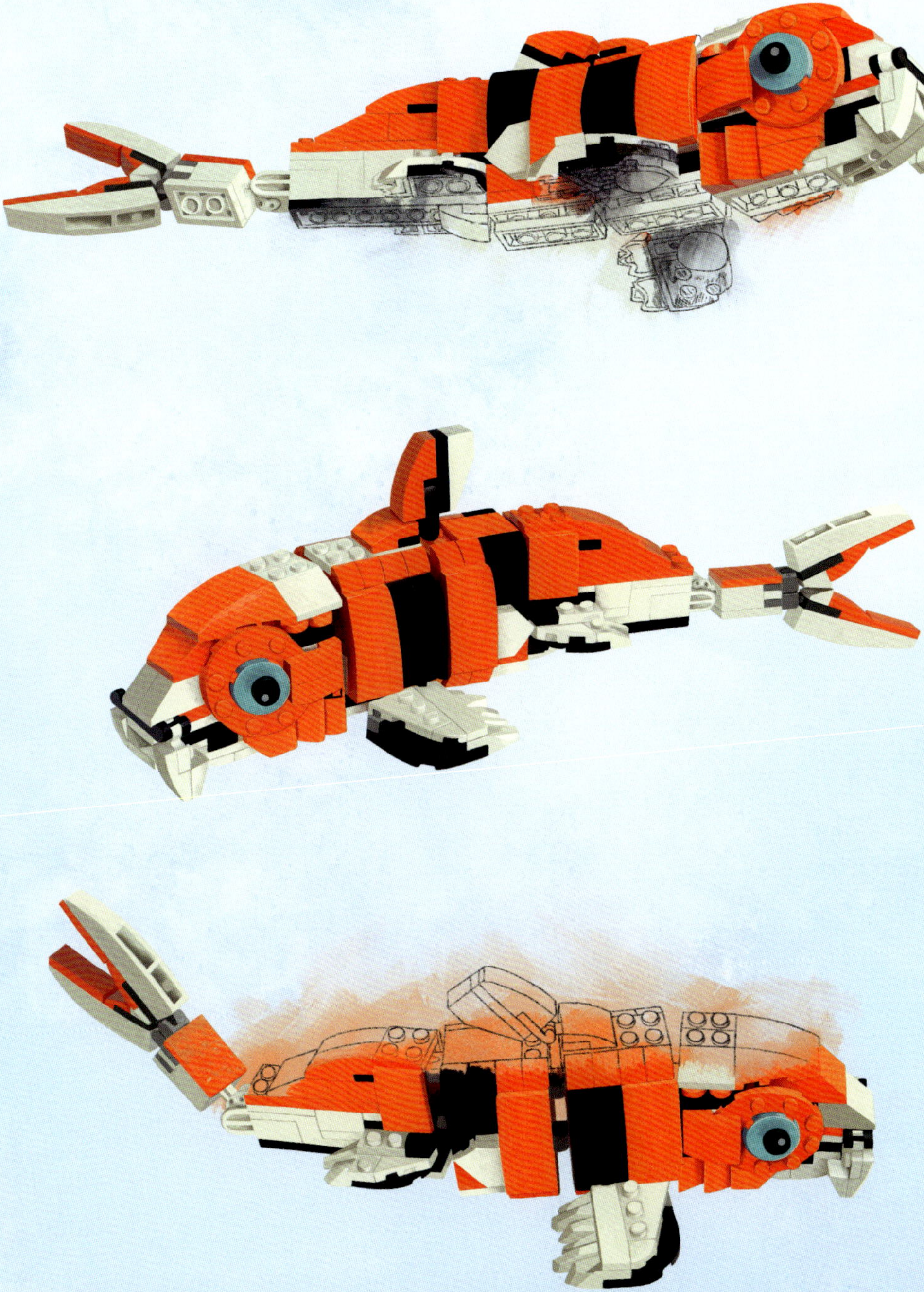

KOI FISH

Cyprinus rubrofuscus

Primary Location: Freshwater and ornamental ponds, water gardens
Primary Food Source: Algae, insects, and human-made koi pellets
Average Length: 24 to 36 in (60 to 90 cm)
Average Weight: 15 to 30 lb (7 to 14 kg)

Koi fish are a type of wild Asian carp. They appear in Japanese history as early as 74 CE, when Emperor Keikō is said to have released them into a pond for viewing in Mino Province. In Japan, systematic breeding of koi fish began in the 1820s, and by 1875 it was a more widespread practice there. After World War II, koi fish breeding expanded beyond Japan into countries like the United States, Indonesia, and South Africa. This has resulted in more than 100 different varieties of koi fish!

- *While koi fish are omnivorous, they have been known to eat food as varied as peas, lettuce, and watermelon. They particularly love rice and corn.*
- *Koi is actually the informal name for this fish and comes from the Japanese name* nishikigoi, *which means "brocaded carp."*
- *Though their average lifespan is 40 years, koi fish reportedly can live for up to 100 years—or even up to 200! Koi are sometimes passed down through generations as family heirlooms.*

KOI FISH

Cyprinus rubrofuscus

BONUS INFO AND FUN FACTS!

Today, koi fish are kept as pets on every continent except Antarctica. In Japan, the koi fish symbolizes luck, prosperity, and good fortune. In Chinese culture, it symbolizes fame, family harmony, and wealth. Some people believe that the fish's different colors signify different meanings. Certain highly coveted koi fish can sell for extremely high prices—the red-and-white carp Kōhaku, for example, can cost hundreds of thousands of dollars. In 2018, a collector purchased the most expensive koi in history for a whopping $1.8 million!

- *One koi fish named Hanako reportedly lived to be 226 years old. Scientists determined her age by examining growth rings on her scales.*
- *During winter, when the water drops below 40°F, koi fish go dormant. Their metabolism slows down, and they spend most of their time at the bottom of the pond until the water warms again.*
- *The rarest type of koi fish is the Kōhaku Tancho—a koi with a white body and a single red spot on its head. Part of what makes this koi so beloved is how closely it resembles the Japanese flag.*

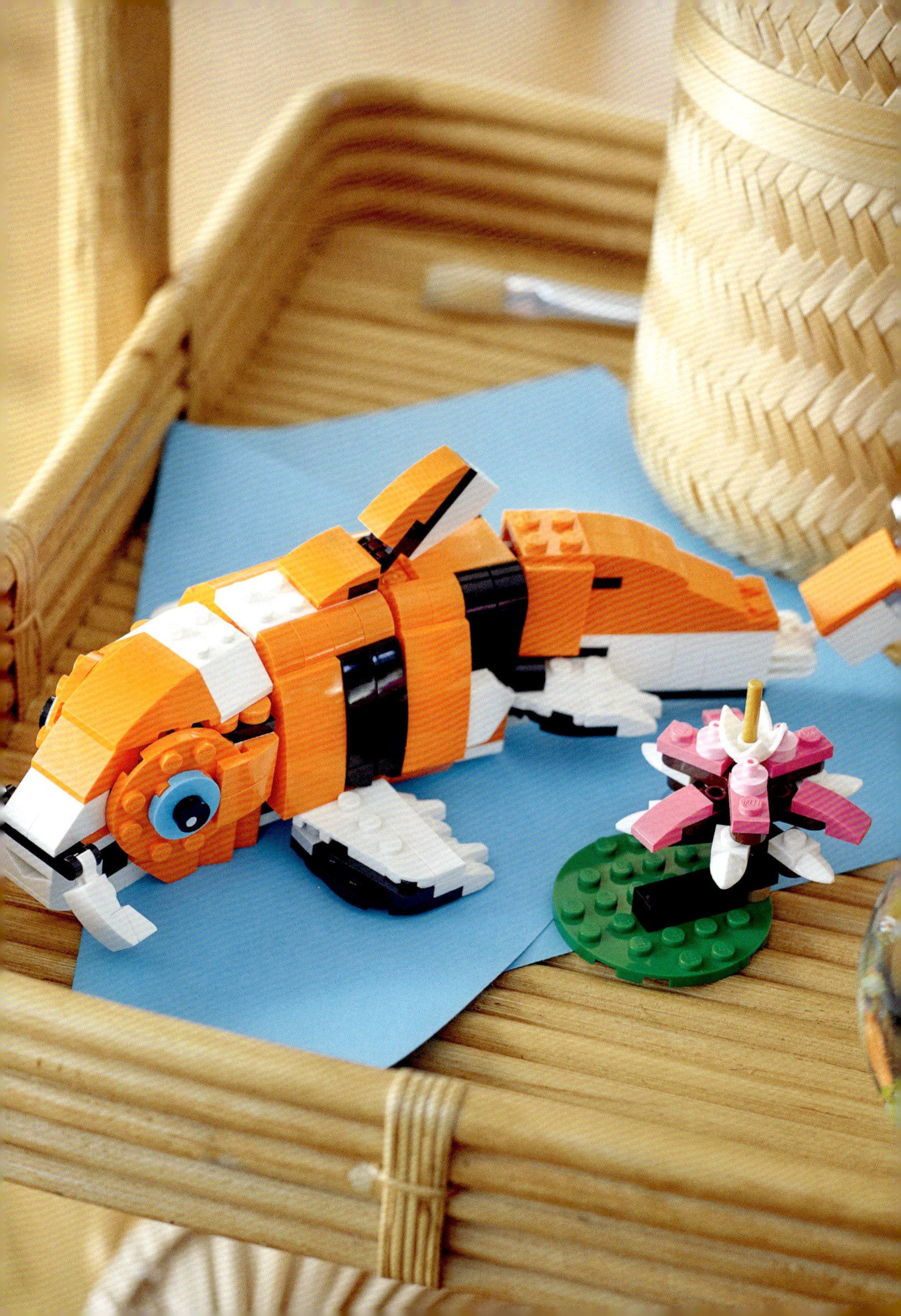

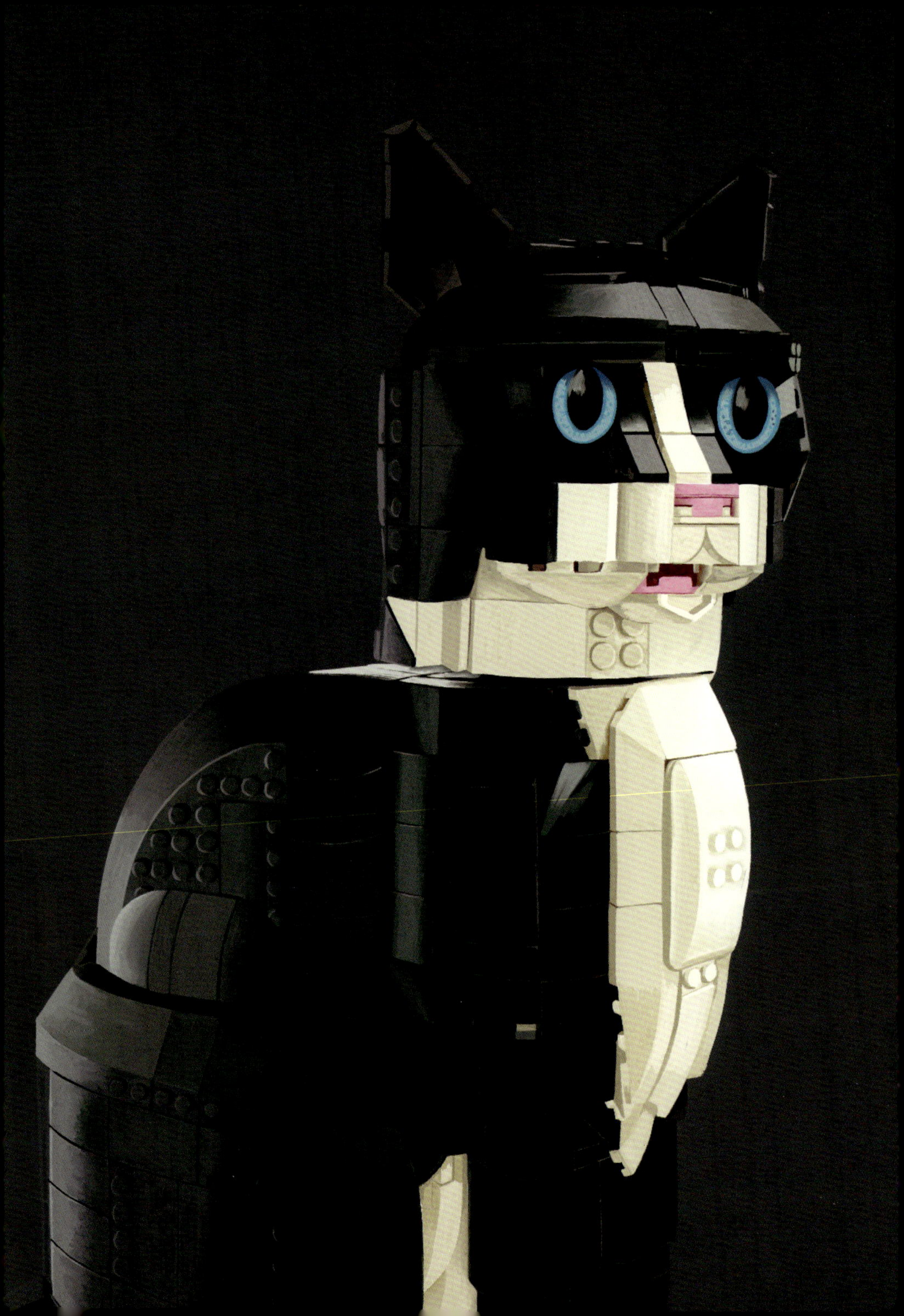

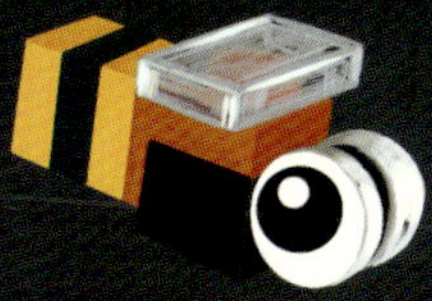

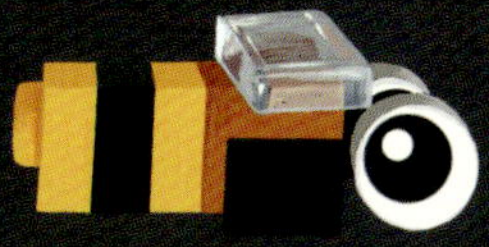

Animal Companions

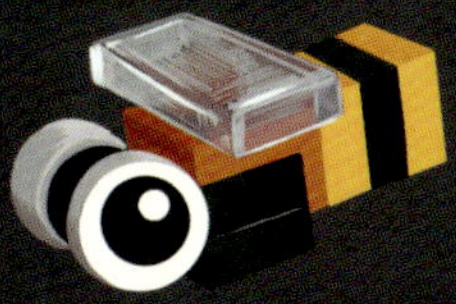

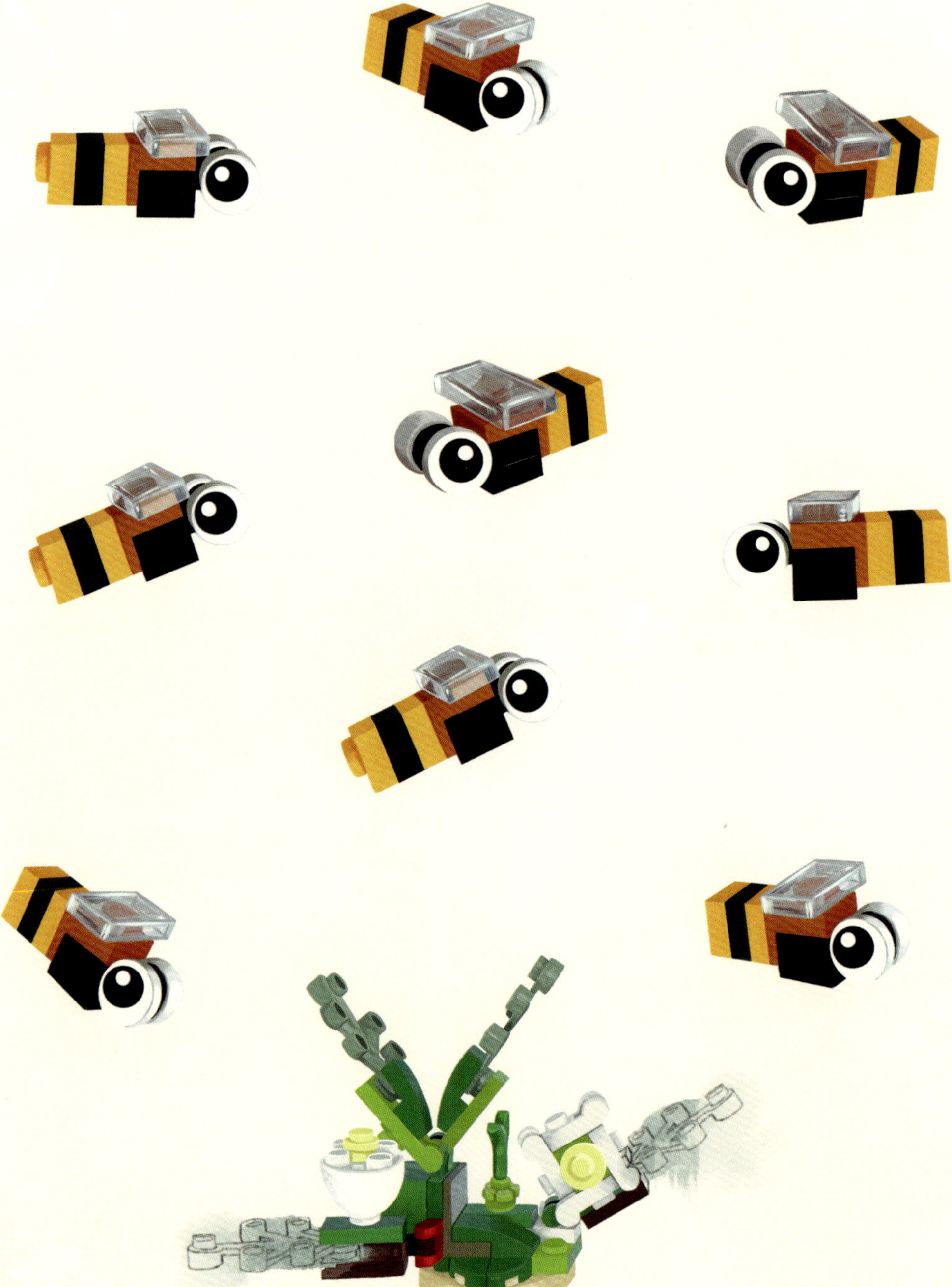

HONEYBEE

Apis mellifera

Primary Location: Worldwide, except Antarctica
Primary Food Source: Nectar and pollen
Average Length: 0.5 to 0.6 in (12 to 15 mm)
Average Weight: About 0.006 oz (0.18 g)

Apis mellifera is the scientific name for the western honeybee, the most common species of honeybee. Bees make honey through a process that requires lots of teamwork. First up are the forager bees, who venture out of the hive to collect nectar and pollen from flowers. Once they land on a suitable flower, they slurp up the nectar and store it in their crop, which is essentially a stomach for the honey. When they return to their hive, they transfer the nectar to a subgroup of worker bees called house bees, who add an enzyme that turns it into glucose and fructose. The bees then put the nectar into wax cells and flap their wings, acting like mini air conditioners to dry the nectar. Once the nectar thickens—voilà! They've made honey!

- *Western honeybees will sting when provoked, but the stinger tears off during the sting, killing the bee in the process.*
- *Forager bees visit anywhere between 50 to 200 flowers in a single journey and can end up carrying their entire body weight in nectar back to the hive. Talk about hard workers!*

HONEYBEE

Apis mellifera

BONUS INFO AND FUN FACTS!

In every hive, there's only one queen bee, which is a bee with a fully developed reproductive system. This bee is responsible for laying eggs in the hive, producing pheromones that keep the colony unified, and founding new colonies if a hive becomes overcrowded. But no bee is *born* a queen. As larvae, all bees are fed something called royal jelly—a diet that is high in protein and low in flavonoids (a natural chemical found in plants). Eventually, worker bees switch to a diet of pollen and nectar, sometimes called bee bread. For a long time, scientists thought that continuing to eat nutrient-rich royal jelly was what made larvae develop into queen bees. However, some more recent studies show the opposite: Chemicals in bee bread have been linked to the development of worker bees, so *not* eating those chemicals is what turns larvae into queens.

- *Western honeybees communicate through dance! They use a round dance—buzzing around in small circles—to tell other bees that food is nearby, and they use a waggle dance to give directions to and the distance of food sources that are farther away.*
- *While there's only one queen bee in the hive, there can be up to 60,000 worker bees at any single time.*
- *A subgroup of worker bees called nurse bees feed and clean the queen bee. Call it the royal treatment!*

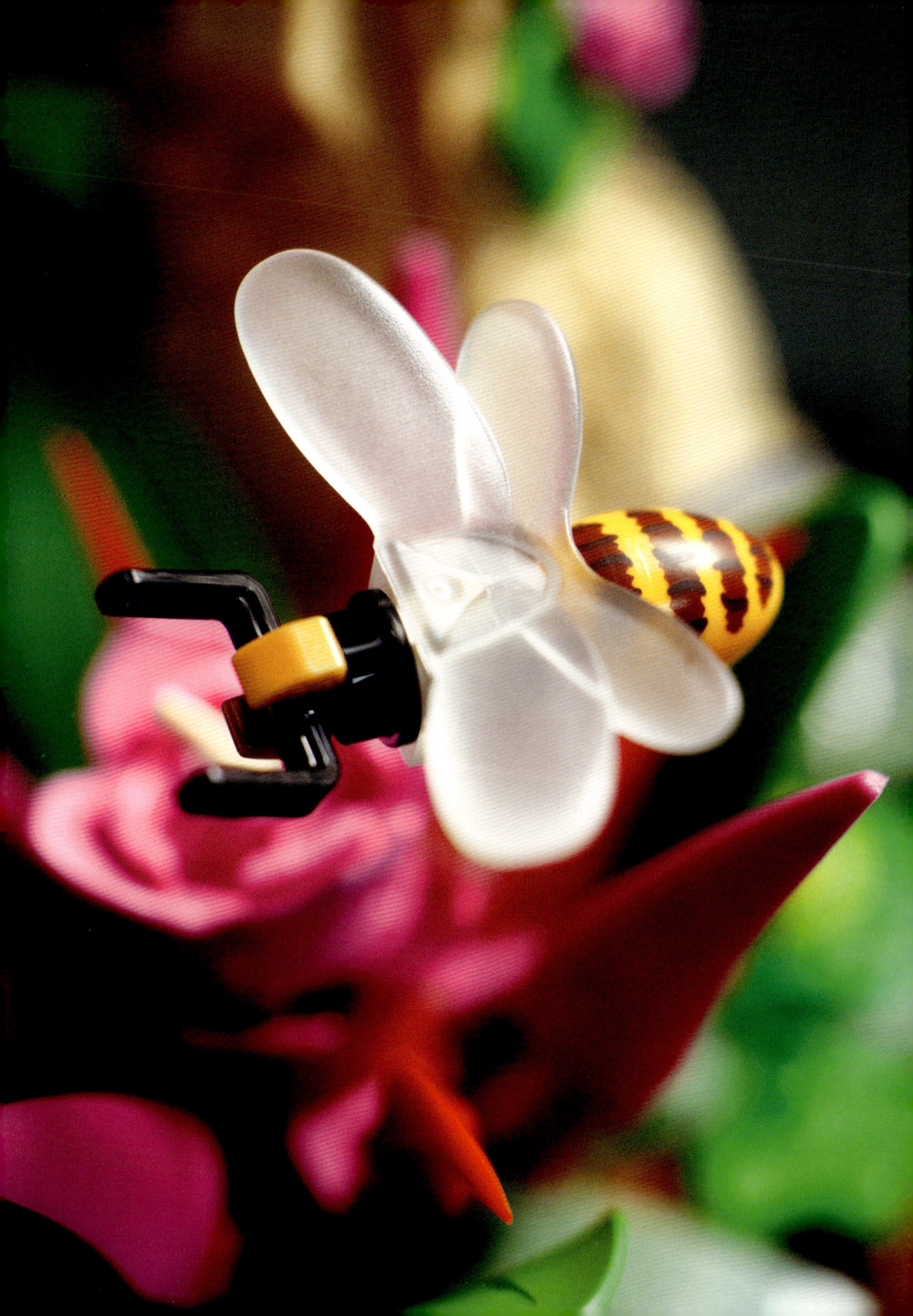

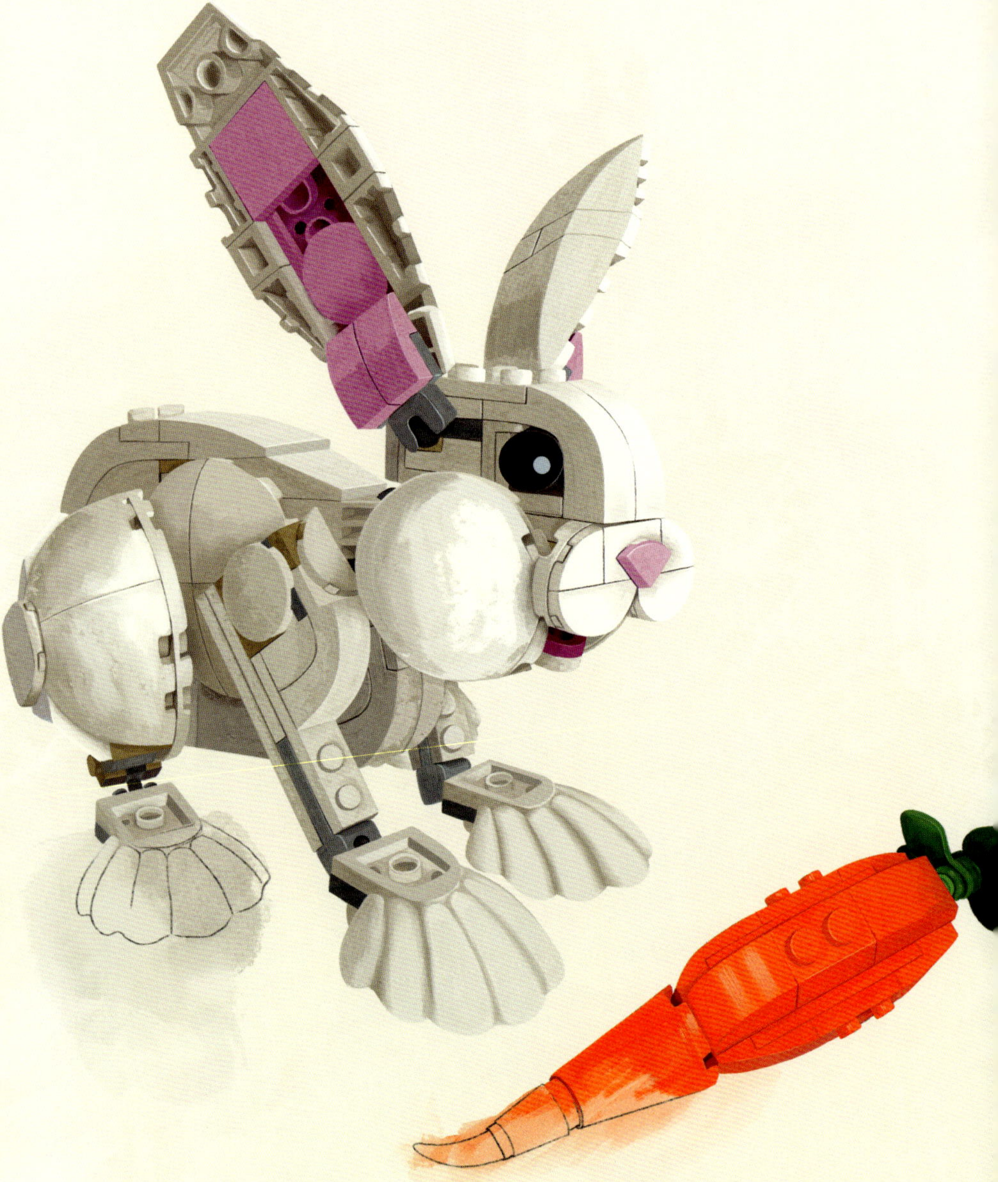

BUNNY

Oryctolagus cuniculus

Primary Location: Worldwide
Primary Food Source: Grasses, leafy plants, and vegetables
Average Length: 8 to 20 in (20 to 50 cm), depending on breed
Average Weight: 2 to 11 lb (0.9 to 5 kg), depending on breed

Bunnies' bodies are built to make them nimble and attuned to their environments. For example, their eyes are positioned on their heads so they can see nearly 360 degrees. The only place they can't see is just below the tip of their nose—so they use both their whiskers and their lips to sense their food and understand what they're about to eat. Their large ears, which can rotate up to 270 degrees, help them hear a wide range of sounds. While humans can hear sounds between 20 and 20,000 Hz (hertz), bunnies can hear sounds between 360 and 42,000 Hz. Their ears also have lots of blood vessels that help with thermoregulation.

- *Bunnies are famous for eating carrots—but actually, they don't eat carrots any more than they eat other plants.*
- *Female rabbits can have as many as six litters a year. With an average of six to eight kits per litter, that's 40 to 50 babies!*
- *Rabbits sleep at night, like humans. Unlike humans, however, they mostly sleep with their eyes open!*

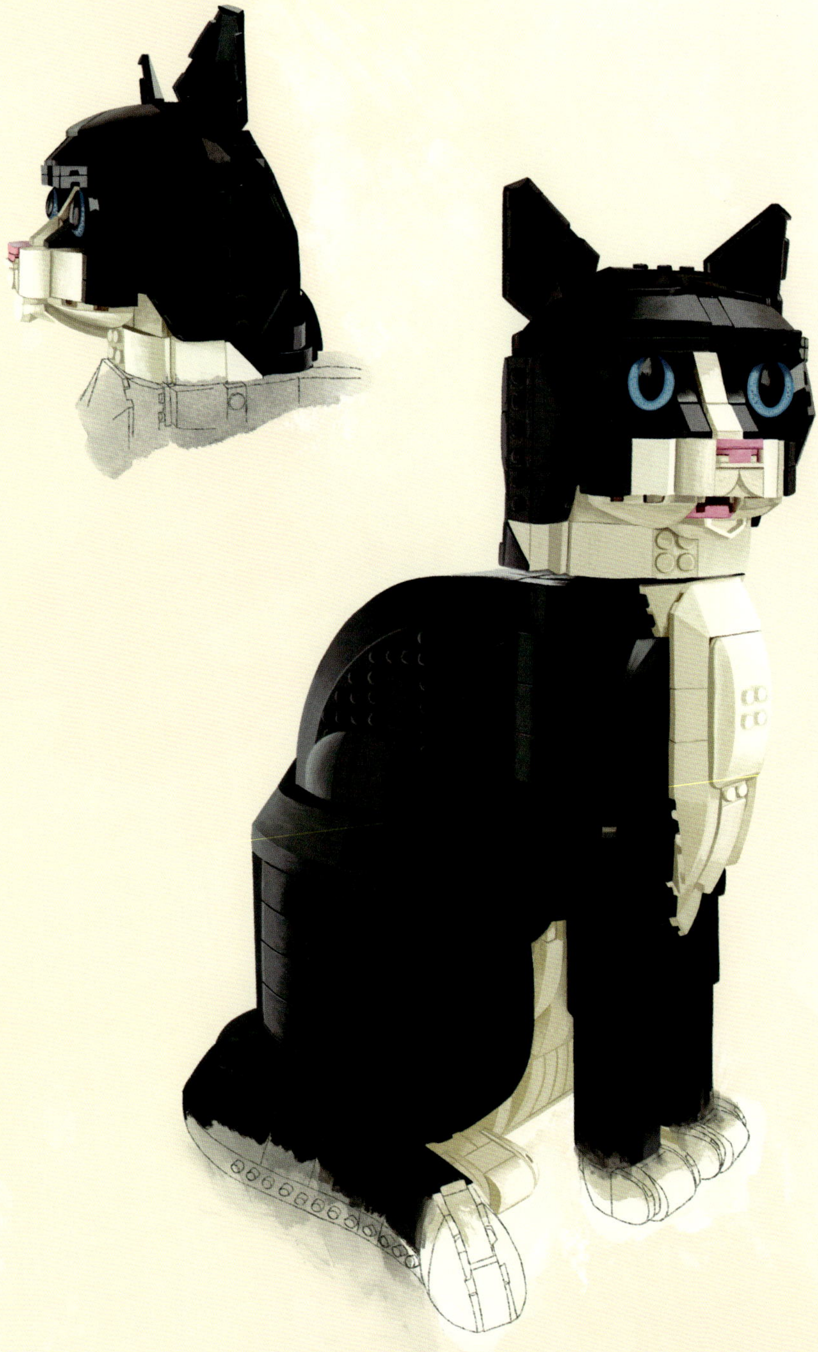

TUXEDO CAT

Felis catus

Primary Location: Domestic environments worldwide
Primary Food Source: Commercial cat food, small mammals, and birds
Average Length: Varies by breed
Average Weight: 7 to 12 lb (3.2 to 5.4 kg)

While dogs were domesticated by humans to serve many different purposes (herding, hunting, guarding, and transportation), cats seem to have invited themselves into human homes more than 10,000 years ago. Over time, people began looking after them, and cats slowly became the wildly popular pets they are today. The skeletons of wild cats and domesticated cats are extremely similar, which suggests that cats did not undergo an intense transformation during domestication.

- *Cats have great night vision. To see in the dark, they need only one-sixth the level of light that humans do!*
- *Cats' ability to see color is not as sharp as ours. They can see blue and yellowish green, but they have trouble telling the difference between red and green.*
- *The next time you observe a cat, see if you can guess their gender based on which paw they use. Male cats tend to prefer using their left paws, while female cats tend to prefer their right!*

TUXEDO CAT

Felis catus

BONUS INFO AND FUN FACTS!

Cats are adored by people around the world—often not in spite of but because of their somewhat detached personalities. This phenomenon has actually been studied: When humans were observed interacting with cats, researchers noticed that people had significant mood boosts after making connections with particularly uncooperative cats.

However, one study suggests that cats can easily recognize the smell of their owner. Researchers gave 30 pet cats plastic tubes with different scents to study their reactions to their owner's scent versus the scents of strangers. They found that the cats spent much longer with the tubes that contained unknown scents.

- *Cats were considered sacred animals and treasured family members in ancient Egypt—so much so that when a cat died, the family would sometimes shave their eyebrows to show their grief!*
- *Cats use their sensitive whiskers to feel the space, air currents, and vibrations around them—just like we use our fingertips! Their whiskers might look like ordinary hairs, but they're actually connected to many blood vessels and nerve endings at the base.*
- *There are over 220 million house cats in the world!*

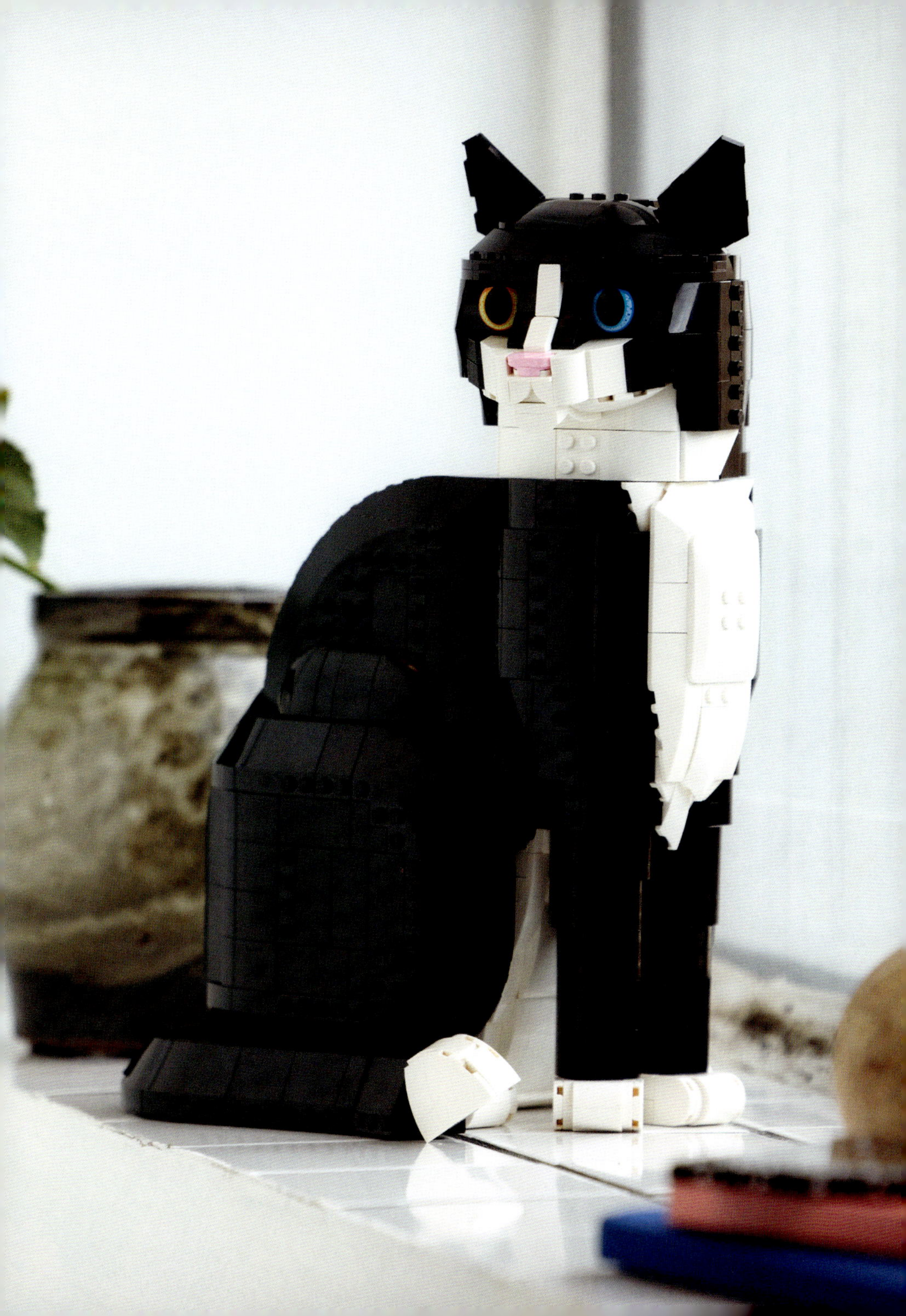

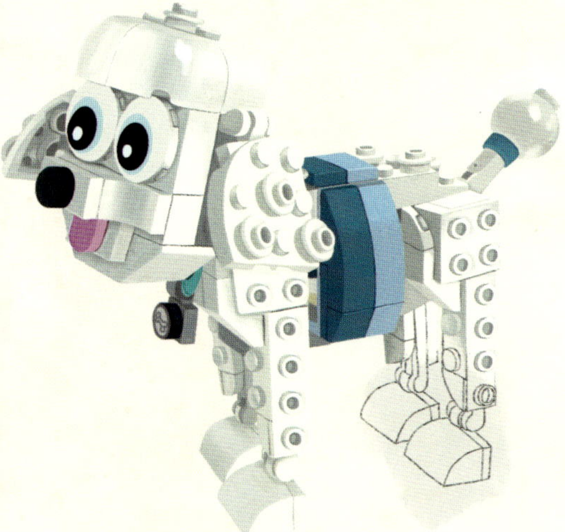

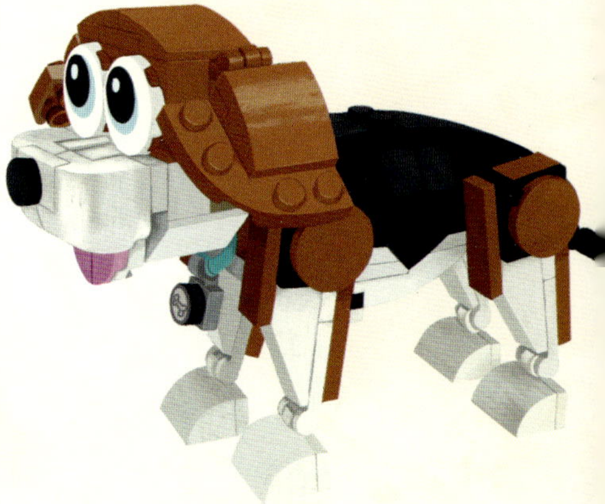

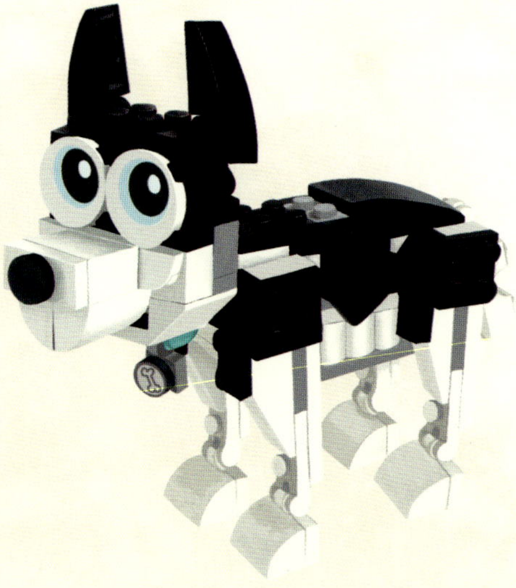

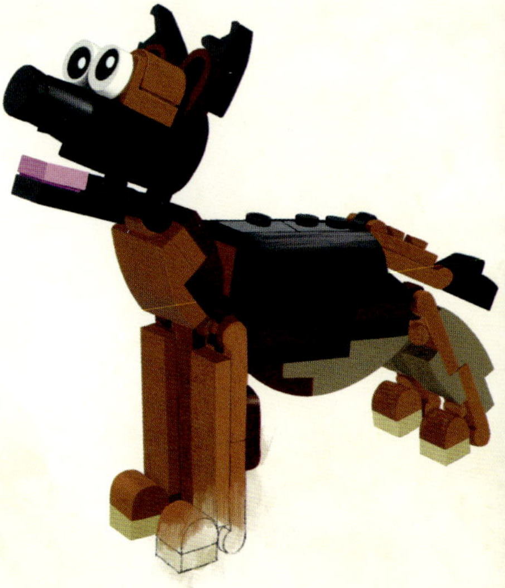

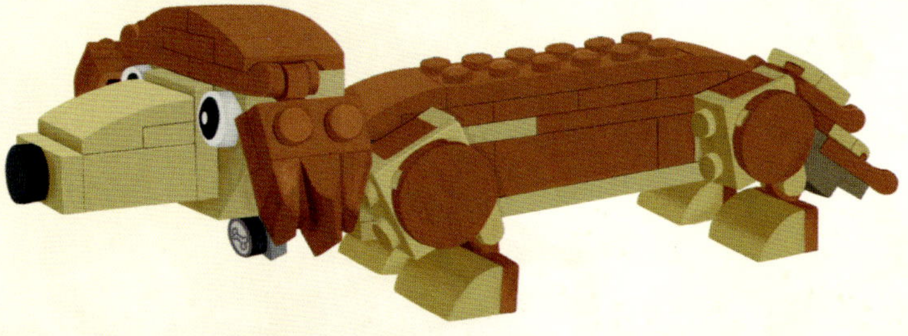

DOGS

Canis lupus familiaris

POODLE, BEAGLE, HUSKY, GERMAN SHEPHERD, DACHSHUND

Dogs are descended from gray wolves. Some studies suggest they were first domesticated as long as 23,000 years ago in Siberia, before eventually becoming the treasured pets we know today.

- *Poodles have been getting unusual haircuts for centuries! In a self-portrait of Rembrandt and his poodle, the back half of the dog's body is shaved.*
- *A beagle's sense of smell is better than most dogs'. In one study, a beagle took less than one minute to sniff out a mouse in a 1-acre field!*
- *In 1925, a group of huskies made a treacherous journey through severe weather to deliver lifesaving serum to the town of Nome, Alaska, during a diphtheria outbreak. They made it, and with every single vial intact!*
- *A German shepherd named Rin Tin Tin was rescued from a battlefield in World War I and went on to become a Hollywood star!*
- *Dachshunds are known for being quite stubborn! E. B. White (author of* Charlotte's Web*) wrote about his dachshund: "When I address Fred I never have to raise either my voice or my hopes. He even disobeys me when I instruct him in something he wants to do."*

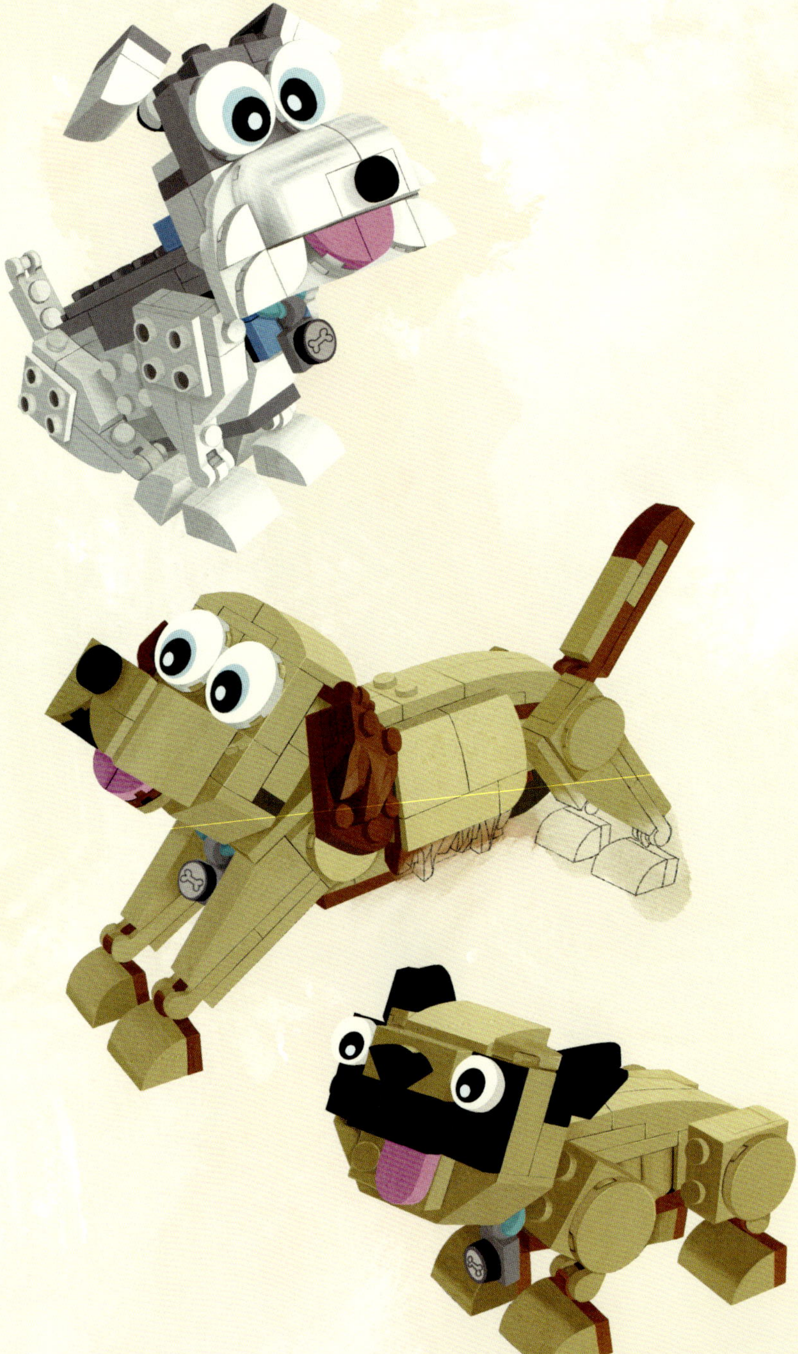

SCHNAUZER

The schnauzer's lineage dates back to 14th-century Germany. In 1503, German artist Albrecht Dürer included a schnauzer in his drawing *Madonna of the Animals*.

- *The schnauzer gets its name from the iconic beard on its muzzle—the German word for "muzzle" is* Schnauze.

LABRADOR

Labradors are loyal, loving dogs who were originally bred to help humans hunt for game. The dogs would retrieve the game—giving them the name Labrador retriever.

- *Labradors are built to be great swimmers! Their tails are sometimes called "otter tails" because they help the dogs steer and propel themselves as they swim. Their coats are also waterproof.*

PUG

Pugs are thought to have originated in China, where they were kept as companions by emperors and royal families. These dogs were so highly coveted that they had their own guards. They eventually gained popularity in European courts as well and arrived in the United States by the 19th century.

- *Even though the Westminster Kennel Club Dog Show in the United States has been around since 1877, a pug has only won Best in Show once! A pug named Dhandy's Favorite Woodchuck took the top prize in 1981.*

The Sets

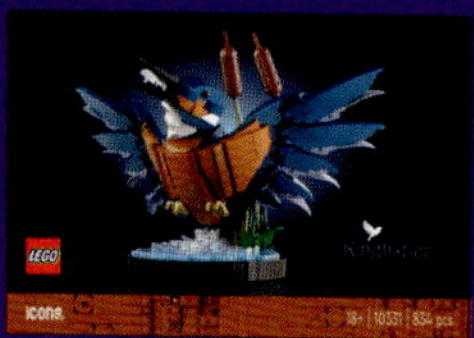

Kingfisher
#10331

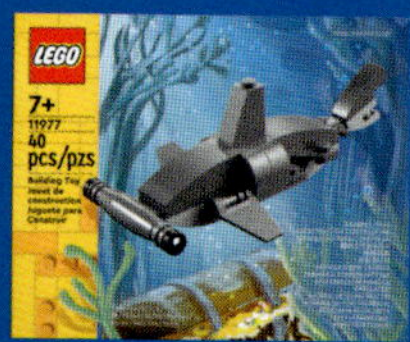

Hammerhead Shark
#11977

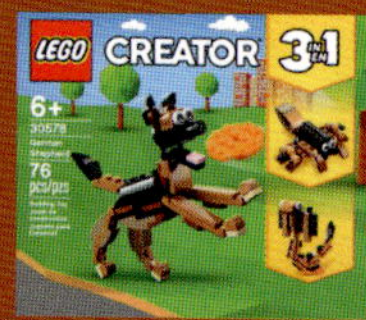

German Shepherd
#30578

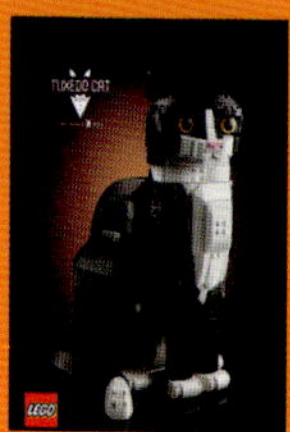

Tuxedo Cat
#21349

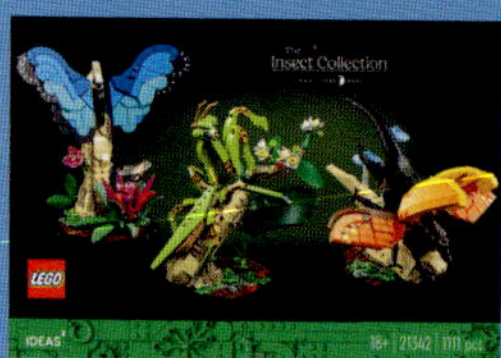

The Insect Collection
#21342

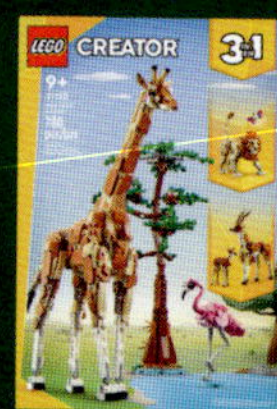

Wild Safari Animals
#31150

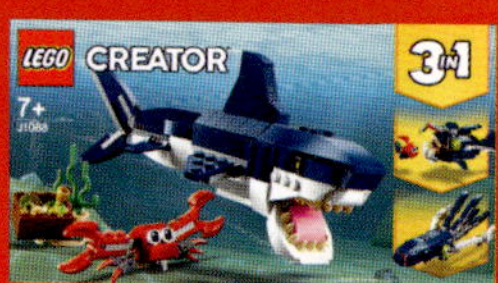

Deep Sea Creatures
#31088

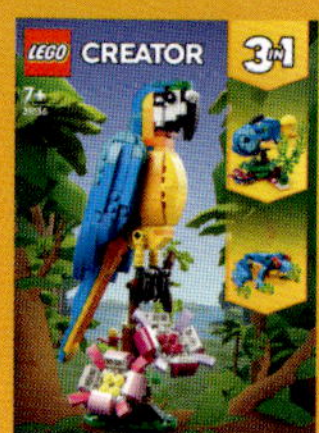

Exotic Parrot
#31136

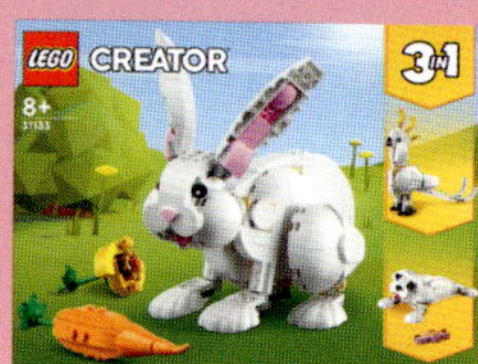

White Rabbit
#31133

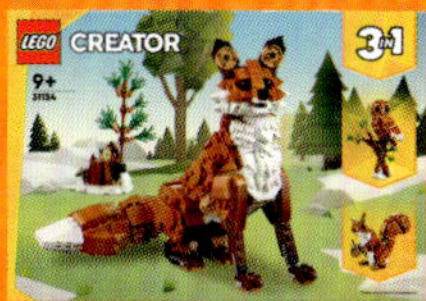

Forest Animals:
Red Fox
#31154

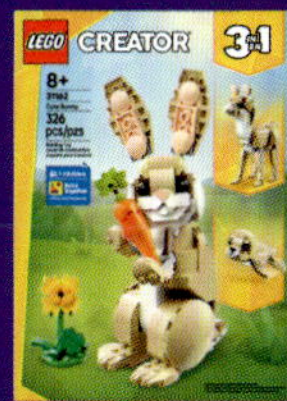

Cute Bunny
#31162

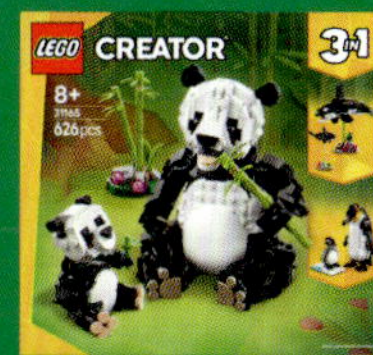

Wild Animals:
Panda Family
#31165

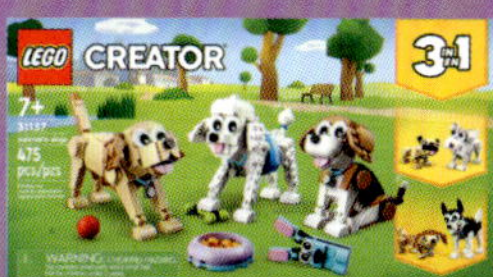

Adorable Dogs
#31137

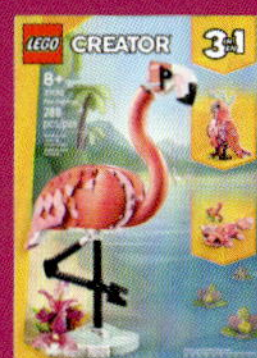

Wild Animals:
Pink Flamingo
#31170

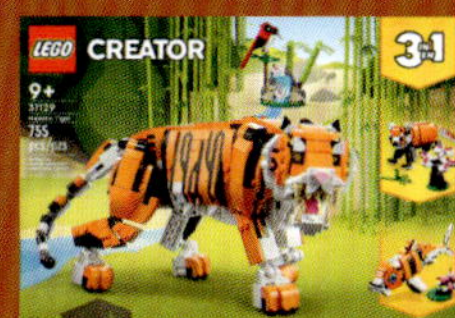

Majestic Tiger
#31129

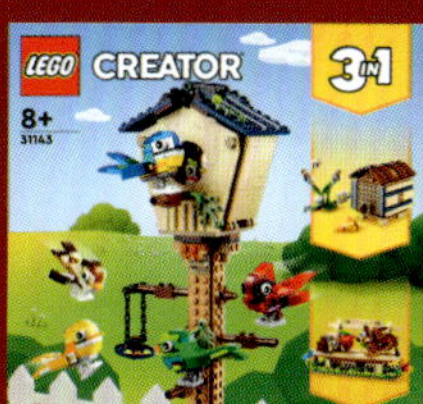

Birdhouse
#31143

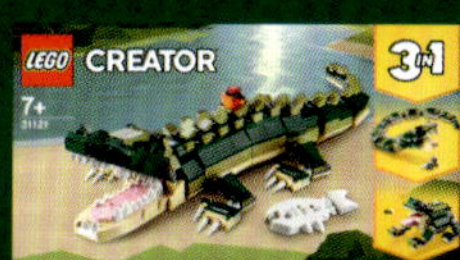

Crocodile
#31121

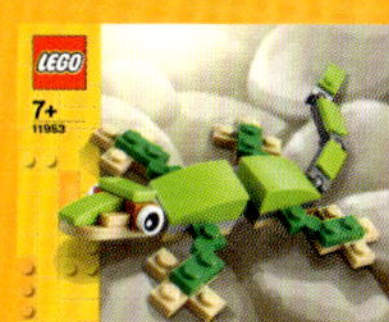

Gecko
#11953

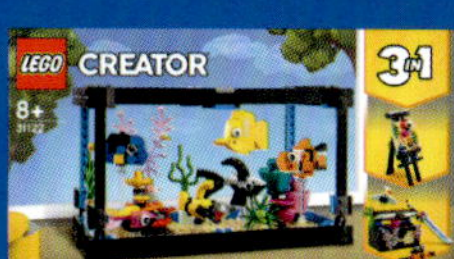

Fish Tank
#31122

Acknowledgments

Thank you to the team of people who provided support to this publication, including Randi Sørensen, Lydia Barram, Ashley Blais, Nina Koopman, Martin Leighton Lindhardt, Nina Pace, Brittany McInerney, Isabel Hinchliff, Sara Schneider, Allison Weiner, Naomi Desai, Perry Crowe, Gabby Boerner, Michelle Clair, Christina Amini, and Aki Neumann.

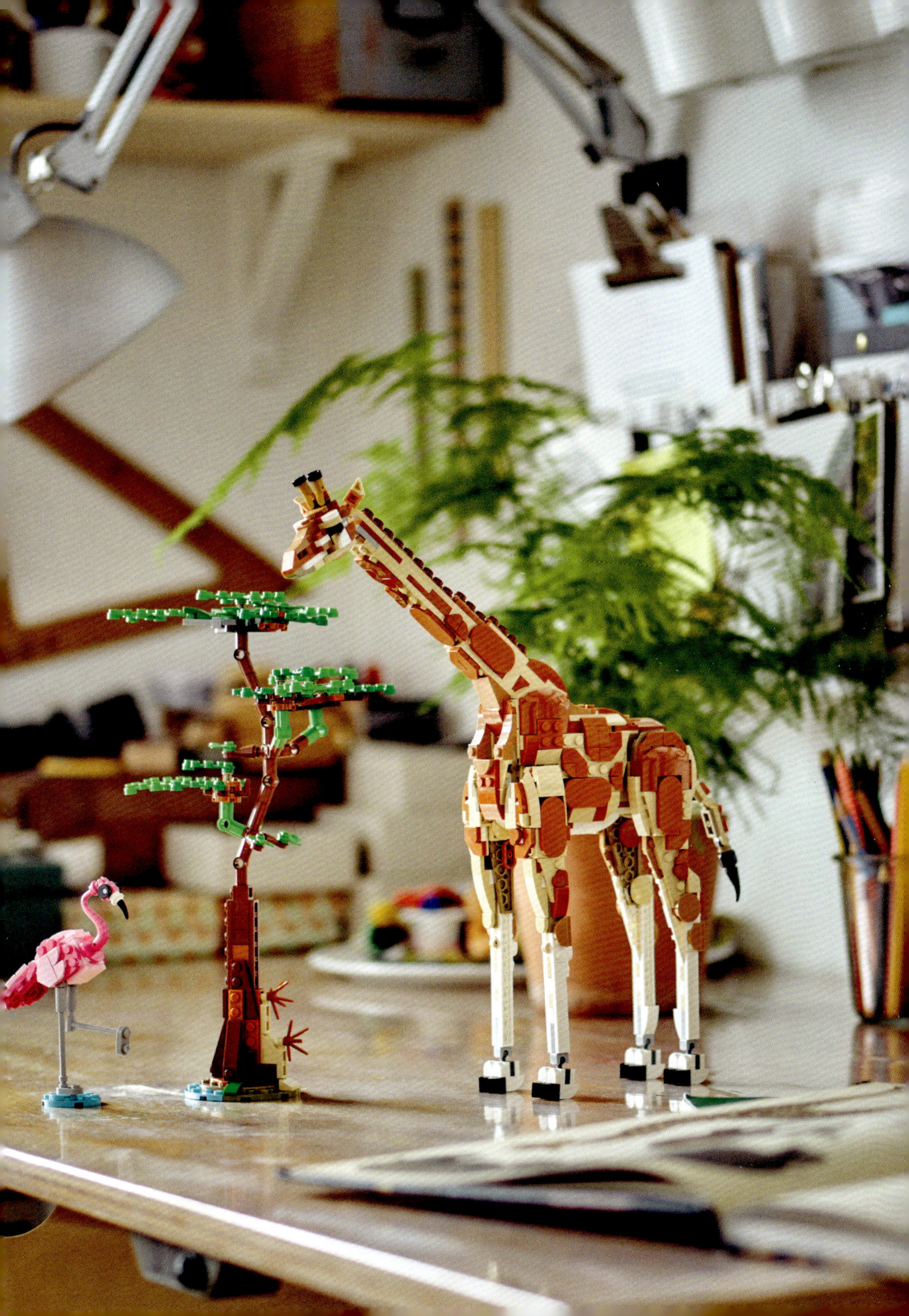

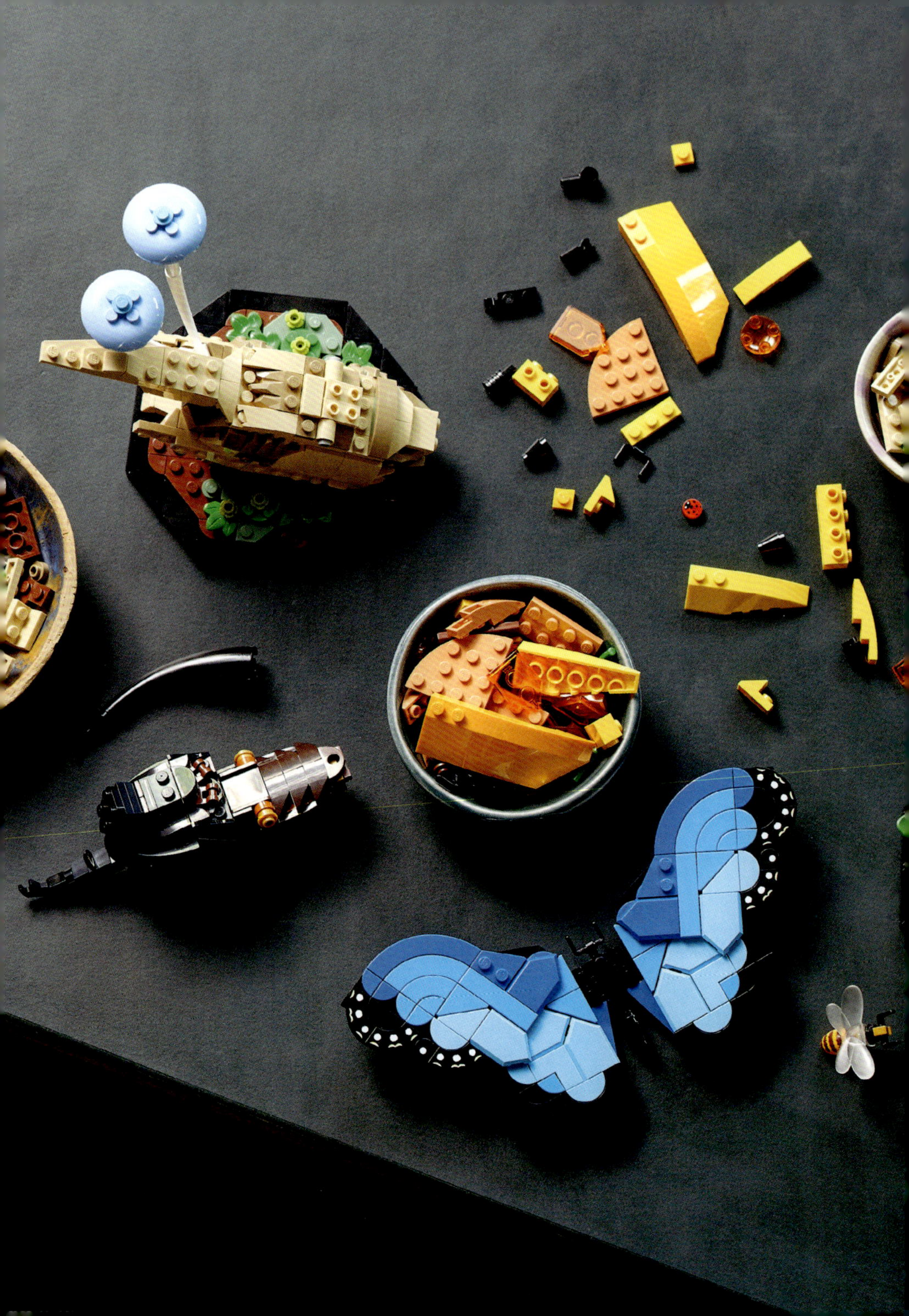

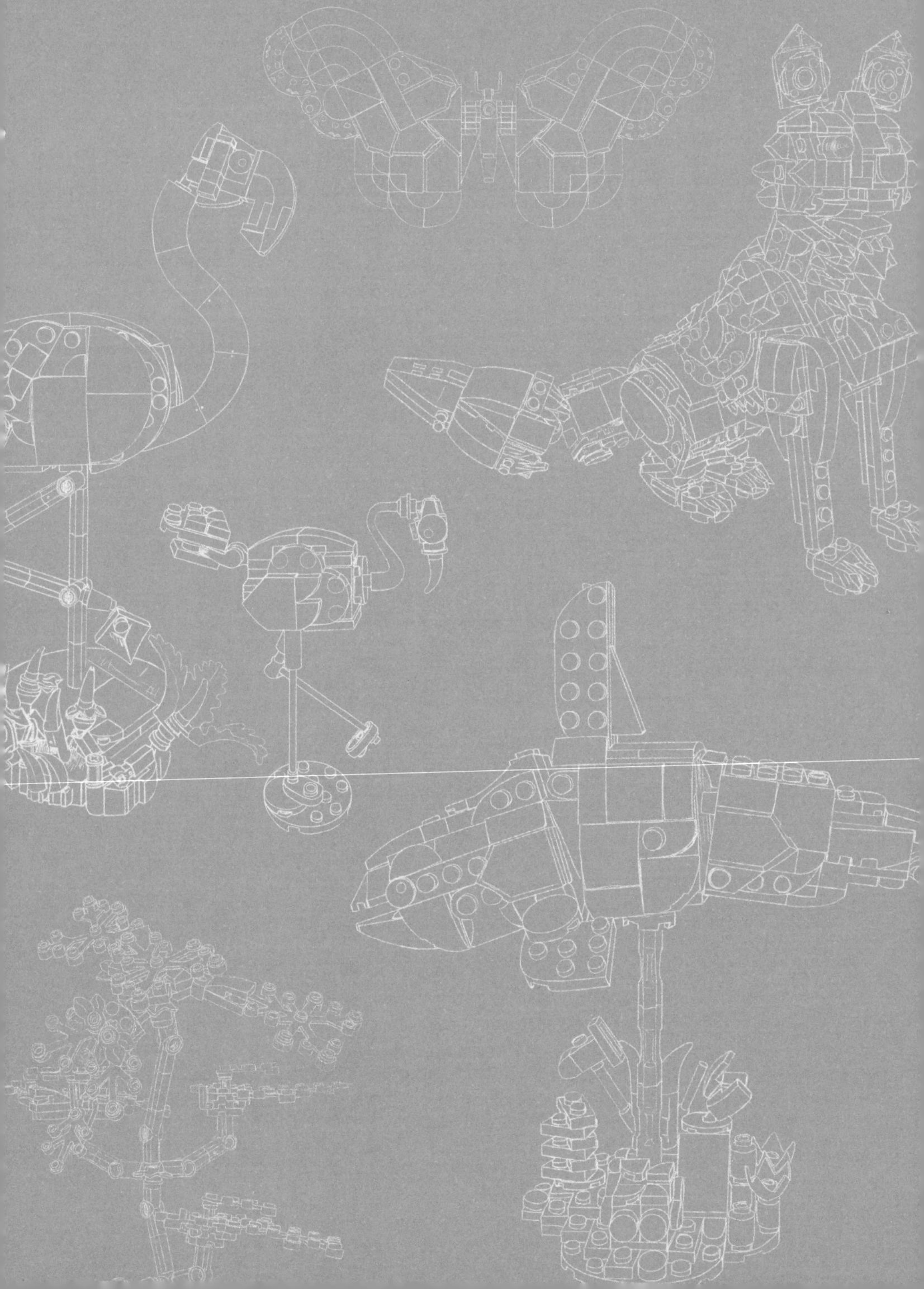